THE BURNOUT BLUEPRINT FOR CAREGIVERS

A STEP-BY-STEP GUIDE TO REDUCING STRESS, SETTING BOUNDARIES AND RESTORING BALANCE - WITHOUT THE GUILT!

ANNIE HARVEY

© **Copyright 2025 - All rights reserved.**

The content contained within this book may not be reproduced, duplicated, or transmitted without direct written permission from the author or the publisher.

Under no circumstances will any blame or legal responsibility be held against the publisher, or author, for any damages, reparation, or monetary loss due to the information contained within this book, either directly or indirectly.

Legal Notice:

This book is copyright protected. It is only for personal use. You cannot amend, distribute, sell, use, quote, or paraphrase any part, or the content within this book, without the author or publisher's permission.

Disclaimer Notice:

Please note that the information contained within this document is for educational and entertainment purposes only. All effort has been executed to present accurate, up-to-date, reliable, complete information. No warranties of any kind are declared or implied. Readers acknowledge that the author is not rendering legal, financial, medical, or professional advice. The content within this book has been derived from various sources. Please consult a licensed professional before attempting any techniques outlined in this book.

By reading this document, the reader agrees that under no circumstances is the author responsible for any losses, direct or indirect, that are incurred due to the use of the information in this document, including, but not limited to, errors, omissions, or inaccuracies.

CONTENTS

Introduction   5

1. UNDERSTANDING BURNOUT AND ITS IMPACT   9
   What's the Difference?   10
   Recognizing the Signs of Burnout   12
   The WHO 2019 Breakdown: Exhaustion, Cynicism, Inefficacy   14
   Why Burnout Feels Inevitable   17
   The Emotional Toll: Isolation and Guilt   19
   Real-Life Stories: Voices from the Heart of Caregiving   21

2. SHIFTING PERSPECTIVES   25
   Embracing Imperfection: Letting Go of Guilt   28
   Finding Gratitude in Daily Challenges   30
   Humor as a Healing Tool   33
   Real-Life Examples: Turning Points and Triumphs   36

3. BUILDING EMOTIONAL RESILIENCE   41
   Mindful Breathing: A Daily Practice of Self-Awareness   45
   Compassion Fatigue: Acknowledging and Overcoming   48
   Transformative Power of Self-Compassion   50
   Exercises for Emotional Resilience   53

4. PRACTICAL SELF-SUPPORT STRATEGIES   57
   Personalized Self-Support Routines   60
   Mindful Moments: Integrating Mindfulness into Busy Days   62
   Digital Detox: Reclaiming Your Peace of Mind   65
   Quick Wins: 10-Minute Self-Support Solutions   67

5. SETTING BOUNDARIES WITHOUT GUILT — 71
   Boundary Setting with Family and Friends — 74
   Balancing Work and Caregiving Responsibilities — 76
   Protecting Your Personal Time — 79

6. ENHANCING RELATIONSHIPS — 85
   Communicating Needs: Opening Up to Loved Ones — 86
   Quality Time: Making the Most of Moments Together — 88
   Managing Empathy Overload — 90
   Rebuilding Connections: Repairing Strained Relationships — 93
   Building a Support Network: Leaning on Others — 96

7. TOOLS FOR LONG-TERM SUCCESS—WITH ANYTHING! — 99
   Weathering the Storm: Strategies for Sustained Resilience — 103
   Adapting to Change: Embracing Flexibility — 105
   Creating a Resilience Toolkit — 107
   Real-Life Stories: Resilient Caregivers — 110

8. MANAGING EMOTIONAL STRESS — 113
   Seeking Help: Removing the Stigma — 115
   Balancing Caregiving and Career: Strategies for Success — 118

9. CREATING A SUSTAINABLE CAREGIVING LIFESTYLE — 123
   Cultivating a Positive Caregiving Environment — 127

Conclusion — 131
References — 135
About the Author — 137

INTRODUCTION

You know that feeling when you're juggling a million things at once, and you're pretty sure you're going to drop at least half of them? Welcome to the world of caregiving! It's like a circus act, except instead of juggling diabolos, you're juggling doctor's appointments, medication schedules, and the occasional emotional breakdown.

Let's be real: caregiving is tough. It's a 24/7 job that comes with no pay, no benefits, and a whole lot of stress. According to the World Health Organization in 2019, burnout is characterized by exhaustion, cynicism, and a sense of hopelessness. Sound familiar? If you're a caregiver, chances are you've experienced at least one (if not all) of these symptoms.

But here's the thing: you're not alone. There are over 40 million unpaid caregivers in the United States alone, over three million in Australia and six million in the UK. Many of them are struggling with the same challenges you are. They're trying to balance work, family, and caregiving responsibilities, all while maintaining their own health and well-being. It's a lot to handle, and it's no wonder that so many caregivers end up burning out.

I know because I've been there. As a caregiver for both of my parents, I've experienced the exhaustion, the guilt, and the overwhelming sense of responsibility that comes with the job. I know how easy it is to get caught up in the never-ending cycle of stress and fatigue.

But I also know that it doesn't have to be this way. After years of trial and error, I've discovered small, simple strategies that can be integrated into daily life to prevent burnout. It's not about trying to do everything perfectly or sacrificing your own needs for the sake of your loved one. It's about finding a balance that works for you and doing it without the guilt.

In this book, we'll explore together the concept of burnout in the context of caregiving, and I'll share some of the strategies that have worked for me and countless other caregivers. We'll cover topics like stress management, self-support, setting boundaries, and more. And throughout it all, I'll be right there with you, offering support, encouragement, and a healthy dose of humor—if I can.

Caregiving is hard, but it's also an incredible opportunity for growth and connection. By learning to manage our stress and prioritize our own well-being, we can not only avoid burnout but also become better caregivers and better versions of ourselves.

So if you're ready to take control of your caregiving journey and find a new perspective on burnout, let's dive in. In the coming chapters, we'll explore practical strategies for managing stress, setting boundaries, and finding moments of joy and resilience in even the toughest of circumstances. I know you may be "over" the word resilience, so I'll explain my take on it in chapter 3.

But before we get started, I want to take a moment to acknowledge you. Yes, you, the caregiver who is doing the best they can with what they have. You, the person who shows up day after day, even when it feels impossible. You, the one who loves so deeply and so fiercely that you're willing to put your own needs aside for the sake of another.

I see you. I hear you. You're enough. You're doing a great job —and thank you.

Now, let's get started on this journey toward a more balanced, resilient, and fulfilling life as a caregiver. It's not going to be easy, but I promise it will be worth it. And who knows? You might even have a little fun along the way.

1

UNDERSTANDING BURNOUT AND ITS IMPACT

Ever had one of those days where everything goes wrong? You're trying to make breakfast, but the toast burns, the phone rings, and the dog decides it's the perfect time to reenact a scene from "Marley & Me." Now, imagine that day, every day—welcome to caregiving. It's a role that requires wearing many hats, often all at once. You're the chef, the nurse, the chauffeur, and the unpaid therapist who occasionally doubles as a human pillow. Sound familiar? If so, you're likely well-acquainted with the relentless whirlpool of emotions that is caregiver burnout. It's not just the fatigue from a long day; it's a more profound exhaustion that seeps into your bones and doesn't shake off with a good night's sleep.

The World Health Organization (WHO) describes it as a syndrome characterized by exhaustion, cynicism, and inefficacy—a triple threat that can leave you feeling like a zombie stumbling through a never-ending episode of "The Walking Dead."

Now, let's get one thing straight: caregiver burnout isn't your run-of-the-mill stress. It's a peculiar beast, like trying to wrestle a crocodile in a kiddie pool. You're not just tired, you're emotionally, physically, and mentally drained. Picture this: after a full day of work, you come home to find the house in chaos—medication schedules to juggle, meals to prepare, and a loved one who depends on you for everything from bathing to just getting through the day.

Unlike general burnout that may find relief through brief respites like a weekend escape, caregiving burnout persists. It extends beyond typical work hours, maintaining its grip even in moments of rest. I invite you to read this book from wherever you're at right now: be it a full-time carer or someone with a loved one who has only recently received a formal diagnosis.

WHAT'S THE DIFFERENCE?

So, what makes caregiving burnout different from the burnout your office buddy might experience after a week of grueling deadlines? For starters, the stakes are higher. You're not just dealing with spreadsheets and emails; you're responsible for another human being's well-being, often without the luxury of clocking out. It's an all-consuming responsibility that can leave you feeling stranded in a sea of never-ending tasks, each more crucial than the last.

The physical exhaustion can be brutal, as caregiving often requires manual labor—lifting, moving, and assisting with daily activities. You're not just tired; you're physically spent, as if you've run a marathon daily, without the medal and cheering crowd.

Emotionally, caregiving burnout is a rollercoaster. You're constantly navigating the highs and lows of someone else's health, mood, and needs. It's like trying to play a game where the rules change daily, and you're expected to keep up without missing a beat. You might find yourself snapping at loved ones or feeling irritable for no apparent reason, except that you're perpetually running on empty.

Mentally, the burnout is just as taxing. The constant vigilance required to ensure that medications are taken, appointments are kept, and unexpected emergencies are handled can leave your brain feeling like a tangled ball of wool.

Caregiving burnout is a unique kind of depletion that blends physical, emotional, and mental exhaustion into a potent cocktail that's hard to swallow. Yet, it's often quietly endured because we caregivers tend to put everyone else first, leaving our own needs on the back burner. It's a reality that can feel isolating—but remember, you're not alone. This book is here to remind you that while caregiving may be challenging, it's also a journey of resilience and growth. And if you're reading this, you're already taking the first step toward reclaiming balance and finding those small, simple strategies that can make a world of difference.

RECOGNIZING THE SIGNS OF BURNOUT

Burnout doesn't just show up one day with a neon sign announcing its arrival. No, it's a sneaky little thing that creeps into our lives almost unnoticed, like an uninvited guest who refuses to leave. It starts subtly, like a slow drip from a leaky tap. You might notice that your energy levels aren't quite what they used to be.

Tasks that once felt like a breeze now seem like Herculean efforts. You wake up after a whole night's sleep yet feel like you've run a marathon. As the days go by, you find yourself growing more irritable. Your patience wears thin, and the most minor things—like a misplaced remote—ignite a spark of frustration. Chronic fatigue sets in, and no amount of coffee seems to cut through the haze. It's like living in a fog, where everything takes twice the effort, and satisfaction seems forever out of reach.

The physical symptoms of burnout are just as insidious. Persistent headaches become your companion, and your muscles feel like they've been wound tighter than a drum. You might notice a tension in your shoulders that never entirely goes away or a dull ache in your back that flares up when you least expect it. Emotionally, you might feel numb, like watching your life unfold from a distance.

You go through the motions, but the joy and connection that once defined your relationships seem to have faded. It's as if someone pressed the mute button on your emotions, leaving you feeling detached from the world around you.

Burnout doesn't just impact your health; it seeps into your daily caregiving tasks, too. You might find yourself forgetting essential appointments or overlooking medications. Your once sharp mind feels sluggish, and your ability to juggle multiple responsibilities falters. As your patience dwindles, you might snap at loved ones or find it harder to muster the empathy and compassion that once came so naturally. Caring becomes a chore, and you feel like you're constantly running on empty. It's a cycle that feeds on itself, leaving you feeling more depleted with each passing day.

To break free from this cycle, it's crucial to cultivate self-awareness and recognize when burnout is creeping in. Take a moment to assess your mental and physical health regularly. Consider setting aside time each week to reflect on your experiences and emotions. Journaling can be a powerful tool for self-reflection, allowing you to track patterns and identify triggers.

Ask yourself questions like, "What drained my energy today?" or "How did I care for myself this week?" These prompts can help you gain insight into your stress levels and identify areas that need attention. By regularly evaluating your stress levels and identifying warning signs, you can take proactive steps to manage burnout before it reaches a tipping point.

THE WHO 2019 BREAKDOWN: EXHAUSTION, CYNICISM, INEFFICACY

Burnout takes center stage in the grand theater of caregiving, and the World Health Organization (WHO) has given us a front-row seat. It's broken down burnout into three dimensions that many of us know all too well: exhaustion, cynicism, and inefficacy.

Imagine a day when your energy tank is running on fumes. Emotional and physical exhaustion hit like a one-two punch. You wake up feeling like you've just completed a triathlon, even though your only feat was managing to get out of bed. Every movement feels heavier, and every task is a mountain to climb. Motivation? Well, that's packed its bags and left town, leaving you to wade through daily activities with the enthusiasm of a sloth on a sleepy Sunday. Sleep promises no sanctuary, as disturbances and insomnia join the party, ensuring you're tossing and turning like a human blender overnight.

As if exhaustion wasn't enough, cynicism sneaks in. It's the grumpy cat of emotions, making everything seem bleak. Your once noble calling of caregiving now feels like you're stuck in an endless loop like Groundhog Day. Frequently, it's the observant eyes of those around you that recognize these signs of cynicism before you become aware of them yourself.

The optimism that fueled your caregiving journey has been swapped for a negative outlook, and suddenly, the glass isn't just half empty, it's bone dry. You find yourself questioning the point of it all, feeling unappreciated, like an unsung hero. Support feels like a distant dream, and the cheerleader squad you once envisioned is nowhere in sight. The stress of the role can lead you into a tailspin of detachment, making you wonder if you're just going through the motions.

Then, there's inefficacy, the sneakiest of them all. Inefficacy often emerges as the most insidious yet least recognized aspect of burnout, a point I frequently emphasize in my keynote presentations globally. Its subtlety and complexity render it less discussed and understood, yet it plays a crucial role in the burnout experience. You start doubting your skills, questioning every decision as if you're starring in your own personal reality show. You compare yourself to others who seem to have it all together, and it feels like you're constantly coming up short.

It's as if everyone else got the memo on how to be a perfect caregiver, and you're left flipping through the pages with no glossary in sight. This insidious self-doubt creeps in, breeding a sense of hopelessness that can be hard to shake.

INEFFICACY CYNICISM EXHAUSTION.

The WHO's breakdown isn't just a diagnostic tool—it's a mirror reflecting the reality that many caregivers face daily. Exhaustion, cynicism, and inefficacy aren't just words—they're lived experiences that can leave you feeling like you're carrying the world's weight on your shoulders.

But recognizing these dimensions is the first step to taking back control. Understanding the enemy is half the battle, and knowing that these feelings are part of a recognized syndrome can offer a glimmer of solace. You're not alone, and you're not imagining things. Burnout is real; acknowledging it is the first step in navigating the storm.

WHY BURNOUT FEELS INEVITABLE

Ever feel like you're stuck on a treadmill that's going nowhere, just running in place with no end in sight? That's what caregiving can feel like. Society has this odd fascination with self-sacrifice, often holding it up as the gold standard for caregiving. We're taught that putting ourselves last is noble, even heroic. But in reality, that mindset is a fast track to burnout.

This expectation doesn't just come from the world around us; it's embedded within us, like an unwelcome guest. We carry this internalized guilt, whispering that we're never doing enough. Add a sprinkle of perfectionism on top, and you have a recipe for disaster. It's like trying to build a house on quicksand. You feel like you should be able to handle it all, but the ground keeps shifting beneath your feet.

Now, add to that the lack of resources and support. It's like trying to build a sandcastle with no sand—frustrating and nearly impossible. You're left feeling like a one-person band, expected to play every instrument without missing a beat. It's no wonder burnout seems like an inevitable guest at the dinner table. The support systems that should catch you when you fall often seem like they're on extended leave. And over the years as I've worked with carers, many say that burnout is just part of the role.

Let's not forget the cycle of overcommitment—our old, familiar frenemy. In the world of caregiving, saying no feels like an extravagance you can't afford. You take on more than you should, juggling tasks like a circus performer, because asking for help feels like admitting defeat. There's a reluctance to delegate, a fear that if you let go of even one responsibility, the whole house of cards will come crashing down. You're scared of letting others down, so you keep adding to your plate, even as it buckles under the weight. It's a vicious cycle, and it's exhausting.

But here's the good news: breaking this cycle is possible. It starts with self-advocacy. Speak up for your needs, even if your voice shakes. You deserve a seat at the table, and your needs are valid. Build a robust support network, one that can weather the storms. Whether it's friends, family, or fellow caregivers, surround yourself with people who understand and who can offer a listening ear or a helping hand.

Remember, asking for help isn't a sign of weakness; it's proof of your strength. You're not in this alone, and together, we can shuffle off the chains of inevitability and step into a world where balance and resilience are more than just buzzwords—they're a reality.

THE EMOTIONAL TOLL: ISOLATION AND GUILT

Imagine yourself as the star of a one-person show, where the audience is perpetually on mute. Welcome to the world of caregiving isolation. When caught up in the whirlwind of caregiving duties, time for social interactions becomes a scarce commodity. Friends' invites gather dust, and your social life becomes a distant memory. It's not that you don't want to connect with others; it's just that the opportunity never seems to present itself between medication schedules and the impromptu symphonies of chaos at home.

Emotional withdrawal becomes second nature, like a defense mechanism against constant demands. You find yourself drifting away from family and friends, not because you want to, but because the exhaustion makes the effort feel insurmountable. It's like you're on an island, surrounded by a sea of responsibilities, with no bridge in sight.

Then there's the guilt, that persistent, nagging feeling that you're not doing enough, even when you're doing everything you can. A relentless shadow lingers, whispering that every hiccup and misstep is somehow your fault. The guilt makes you feel responsible for everything that goes wrong, as if you should have a crystal ball to predict every possible outcome.

Accepting help feels like admitting defeat, and you're left carrying the world's weight on your shoulders because asking for assistance feels like another luxury you can't afford. This guilt isn't just exhausting; it's debilitating. It chips away at your mental health, leading to anxiety and even depression. Constant self-criticism and self-doubt become your daily companions, eroding your confidence and leaving you trapped in a never-ending cycle of inadequacy.

But what if I told you there's a way to break free from isolation and guilt? Enter peer support groups, your new best friend. Finding a group of like-minded individuals who understand the unique challenges of caregiving can be a game-changer. It's a space where you can vent, share, and laugh (yes, laugh) at the absurdities of caregiving without fear of judgment.

Beyond support groups, validation becomes a powerful tool. Allow yourself to acknowledge and validate your struggles, recognizing that what you're doing is incredibly hard and feeling overwhelmed is okay. It's not about wallowing; it's about giving yourself permission to be human. Practicing self-compassion can also work wonders. Replace that inner critic with a voice of kindness that forgives and nurtures. Remember, you're doing your best, and that's more than enough. By treating yourself with the same kindness you offer others, you'll find that the weight of guilt begins to lift, allowing room for empowerment and resilience.

REAL-LIFE STORIES: VOICES FROM THE HEART OF CAREGIVING

Let's take a moment to step into the shoes of caregivers from all over the world, each walking their own winding path. Meet Sarah, a nurse from London who spends her days tending to patients and her evenings caring for her partner with Lewy Body Dementia. Her life is a juggling act between hospital shifts and home duties, often leaving her feeling like she's running a marathon with no finish line.

Then there's Liam, from Sydney, who balances his job as an IT consultant with caring for his aging mother. His story is one of innovation, using revolutionary technology to help manage his mother's care while he's at work. He's a pioneer, showing us how to weave modern solutions into age-old problems.

In the United States, we find Maria, a "sandwich generation" caregiver. Not only does she look after her children, but she also tends to her mother, who has Parkinson's. Her days are filled with school drop-offs, doctors' appointments, and late-night homework help. It's a delicate dance of priorities, where the stakes are high, and the rewards often feel out of reach. Yet, Maria finds resilience in her community, a neighborhood support group that gathers every Thursday night to share stories, laughs, and sometimes tears. It's a haven where empathy reigns and the shared experiences form the glue that holds them together.

Despite their varied backgrounds, these caregivers share common threads. They all juggle caregiving with full-time work, and they all face unexpected challenges—whether it's a sudden health crisis or an emotional breakdown. These stories reflect the universal struggle of balancing personal and professional lives while being the primary support for someone else. However, they also highlight these caregivers' remarkable strategies to avoid burnout. Sarah, for instance, carves out time every morning for yoga. This ritual centers her before the chaos of the day begins. Liam leverages technology, using apps to remind him of medication schedules and appointments, ensuring nothing slips through the cracks.

These narratives aren't just tales of hardship; they are stories of triumph. Each caregiver, in their own way, finds methods to cope and even thrive amidst the storm. They exemplify the strength and creativity it takes to navigate the caregiving landscape. They show that while the road may be challenging, it's not insurmountable. These stories remind us that within each caregiver lies an extraordinary ability to adapt, grow, and find hope in the most challenging circumstances.

As we conclude this exploration into the world of caregiving, remember that these voices echo the shared experiences of many. They remind you that you are part of a vast community, where understanding and support are just a conversation away. You are not alone, and through

these stories, we find solidarity and strength. They teach us that while caregiving is demanding, it's also an opportunity to connect deeply with others and ourselves. Take heart in these tales, and know that you, too, have the power to navigate this path with courage and resilience.

2

SHIFTING PERSPECTIVES

Imagine you're standing at the edge of a great forest. The path ahead is tangled and overgrown; you can't see where it leads. You might feel a bit like this every day as a caregiver—lost in the dense thicket of responsibilities, searching for a way through. But what if you saw this forest as a landscape of possibilities instead of seeing it as an impenetrable obstacle? Despite all its challenges, caregiving is not just a burden; it's a chance to grow, develop new skills, and discover strengths you never knew you had.

Let's start with patience, which, if I'm being honest, wasn't exactly my strong suit. But caregiving has a funny way of teaching you patience, whether you like it or not. It's in those moments when you're waiting for an elevator that seems to have forgotten its job, or when you're explaining, for the hundredth time, why eating cookies for dinner isn't the best idea.

These daily tasks build patience in a way no meditation app can. And then there's empathy, which blooms in the most unexpected places. When caring for someone else, you start seeing the world through their eyes. You develop emotional intelligence that allows you to connect deeply with others, understanding their joys and sorrows with a kind of clarity that's both humbling and profound.

Now, let's talk about that pesky negative self-talk that likes to creep in when you least expect it. You know, the little voice that says, "You're not doing enough," or "You're not cut out for this." It's time to flip the script. Instead of saying "I have to," try saying "I get to." It's a simple change but shifts the focus from obligation to opportunity. It's a reminder that caregiving is a choice, and with that choice comes the chance to make a difference. Reframing your thoughts can cultivate a positive narrative emphasizing growth and possibility rather than stress and frustration.

Caregiving is like a crash course in life skills. You become a master multitasker, juggling appointments, medications, and meals with the agility of a circus performer. Your time management skills rival those of a CEO as you learn to squeeze every drop out of each day.

Conflict resolution becomes second nature, as you negotiate everything from bedtime routines to family dynamics. These skills are not just valuable for caregiving; they're transferable to every area of life. Whether it's managing a team at work, organizing a community event, or simply navigating the chaos of daily life, the skills you hone as a caregiver are invaluable.

But here's the best part: You have the power to rewrite your story. You're not just a caregiver but the author of your narrative. Take control of the pen and find meaning in your journey. Create a vision board that captures the positive outcomes you hope to achieve. Use personal storytelling exercises to reflect on your experiences and identify moments of growth and learning. Remember, you're not just surviving; you're thriving. Each day presents a new opportunity to learn, grow, and transform the ordinary into the extraordinary.

Personal Storytelling Exercise

Grab a notebook or open a new document on your device. Reflect on a recent caregiving experience that challenged you. Write about it, focusing on your emotions, actions, and reflections. Then, identify one positive outcome or lesson learned from this experience. How did it contribute to your growth or understanding? This exercise is designed to help you see the silver lining and appreciate the journey of personal development that caregiving offers.

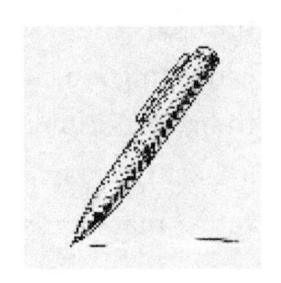

EMBRACING IMPERFECTION: LETTING GO OF GUILT

Imagine standing in front of a mirror that reflects not just your image but every expectation you've ever had of yourself. Now, imagine that mirror shatters, and you're left with the pieces of who you really are—imperfect and beautifully human.

As caregivers, we often hold ourselves to impossible standards, striving for a perfection that, quite frankly, doesn't exist. It's like balancing a dozen spinning plates on sticks whilst standing on one leg. Things will wobble, sometimes they'll crash—and that's okay. Embracing imperfection is recognizing that mistakes are not failures but steppingstones to something greater. Each slip-up, each forgotten appointment, is a chance to learn, adapt, and grow.

Societal expectations weave a web of guilt and inadequacy that can feel suffocating. The media often portrays caregiving as an act of saintly devotion, where caregivers glide through their duties with a serene smile and never a hair out of place. But real life isn't a Disney movie, and those portrayals do a disservice to the grit and resilience it takes to care for another human being day in and day out.

Cultural narratives often glorify selflessness to the point of martyrdom, leaving you feeling like you should be able to do it all without breaking a sweat. Add financial stress and the lack of support to the mix, and you've got a recipe for burnout that no amount of yoga or chamomile tea can soothe.

So, how do we reduce this guilt that clings to us like a stubborn piece of lint? It starts with setting realistic expectations for ourselves. You're not a superhero, and no one expects you to be. Allow yourself to prioritize, delegate, and say no when needed. Practice self-compassion by treating yourself with the same kindness and understanding you give to others. I'm not saying this is easy, by the way. Forgive yourself for the times you fall short, and celebrate the times you get it right. Embrace self-acceptance by acknowledging your strengths and weaknesses, understanding that they're simply parts of the whole.

If you're into them, daily affirmations can be a powerful tool in this journey. Stand in front of a mirror each morning and tell yourself something positive. "I am doing my best, and that is enough." "I am worthy of love and care." It might feel silly at first, but words hold power; over time, they can reshape how you see yourself.

Journaling can also help you track your growth and understand your emotions. Write about your day, your struggles, and your triumphs. Explore what triggers your guilt and how you can address it. Remember, the goal isn't to be perfect; it's to be present, to show up for yourself and those you care for with authenticity and concern.

In this dance of caregiving, there will be missteps. You'll stumble, laugh, and sometimes cry. But through it all, remember that you are enough, just as you are. Imperfections and all, you are doing something remarkable—you're caring, loving, and learning. And that, my friend, is more than enough.

FINDING GRATITUDE IN DAILY CHALLENGES

Picture this: amidst the chaos of caregiving, you find yourself in a rare moment of peace, where the world slows down and you can actually hear your thoughts. Within these moments, gratitude can blossom, offering a fresh perspective on the demanding role you play. Practicing gratitude isn't just about saying thank you or counting your blessings; it's about actively seeking out those tiny, often overlooked moments of joy and appreciation that can transform your day-to-day experience.

A gratitude journal can be a simple yet effective way to bring these moments to light. Each evening, take a few minutes to jot down things you're thankful for—the way the sunlight danced through the window or the unexpected smile from a stranger at the grocery store. In fact, if it's too hard to be thankful every day, then ask yourself one question: "What made me smile today?" Over time, these entries become a collection of positivity, a reminder that there's always something to cherish even in the most challenging times.

It's not just about personal reflections, though. Gratitude letters can be a heartfelt way to express appreciation to those who support you. Writing a note to a friend who always picks up the phone when you call or to a neighbor who checks in on you can reinforce those connections and remind you that you're not alone in this. These letters don't have to be long or elaborate; a simple, sincere message can go a long way in strengthening your support network and lifting your spirits. Plus, it gives the recipient a little boost of happiness, which we all could use a bit more of.

Now, let's talk about those little victories: celebrating them is crucial. Maybe you managed to coordinate a smooth morning routine without significant hiccups, or perhaps you successfully navigated a difficult conversation gracefully. These successes, no matter how small, deserve recognition. Share these moments with your loved ones. Describe the accomplishment you felt when you finally got the hang of a new caregiving technique or the joy of seeing your loved one smile after a tough day. Celebrating these moments with others can foster a sense of community and shared triumph.

The psychological benefits of gratitude are well-documented. Studies show that cultivating gratitude can increase happiness and contentment, reducing stress and anxiety. By focusing on the positive aspects of your life, you can shift your mindset from scarcity to abundance. This isn't just feel-good fluff—research indicates that gratitude can lower stress levels and improve mental health, enhancing resilience and overall well-being. It's like a mental workout, except you're flexing those positivity muscles instead of your biceps and glutes.

Incorporating gratitude into your daily routine doesn't have to be a daunting task. Start with a mindful gratitude walk. As you stroll through your neighborhood or a local park, take note of the things you're grateful for—the chirping of birds, the vibrant colors of the flowers, the gentle breeze on your skin. Allow yourself to be fully present in these moments, letting gratitude wash over you like a soothing balm.

Another idea is to create a gratitude jar for your household. Encourage family members to jot down things they're grateful for on slips of paper, adding them to the jar over time. On days when the weight of caregiving feels heavy, dip into the jar and read those notes to remind yourself of the abundance in your life.

If "I'm grateful for…" feels too challenging some days, try another approach. Reflect on three things that you enjoyed today. These could be as simple as a perfectly brewed cup of coffee or a witty comment from a friend. The key is to focus on the positive, allowing these moments to shine through the clutter of daily stress. In doing so, you'll find that gratitude isn't just a practice—it's a lifeline, a way to navigate the complexities of caregiving with a little more grace, and perhaps a little more joy too.

HUMOR AS A HEALING TOOL

Picture this: you're knee-deep in the daily grind of caregiving, racing against time as you juggle a thousand tasks. Suddenly, the cat decides to knock over a glass of water right as you're trying to convince your loved one that socks are not hats. (Yes, my dad used to do this and it reminded me of the famous book "The Man Who Mistook His Wife for a Hat," by Oliver Sacks.)

You could cry, but instead, you laugh. It's the kind of belly laugh that makes your sides hurt, and your worries melt away, even if just for a moment. Humor has this magical ability to take the edge off life's sharp corners, offering a much-needed dose of relief when the going gets tough. It's like a mental reset button that allows you to step back, breathe, and see the absurdity in the chaos.

Ever heard of laughter yoga? It's a real thing, and it's just as delightful as it sounds. Imagine a room full of people, all laughing together, not because of a joke, but because laughter is infectious. It's a practice that combines laughter exercises with yoga breathing, creating an atmosphere where joy takes center stage.

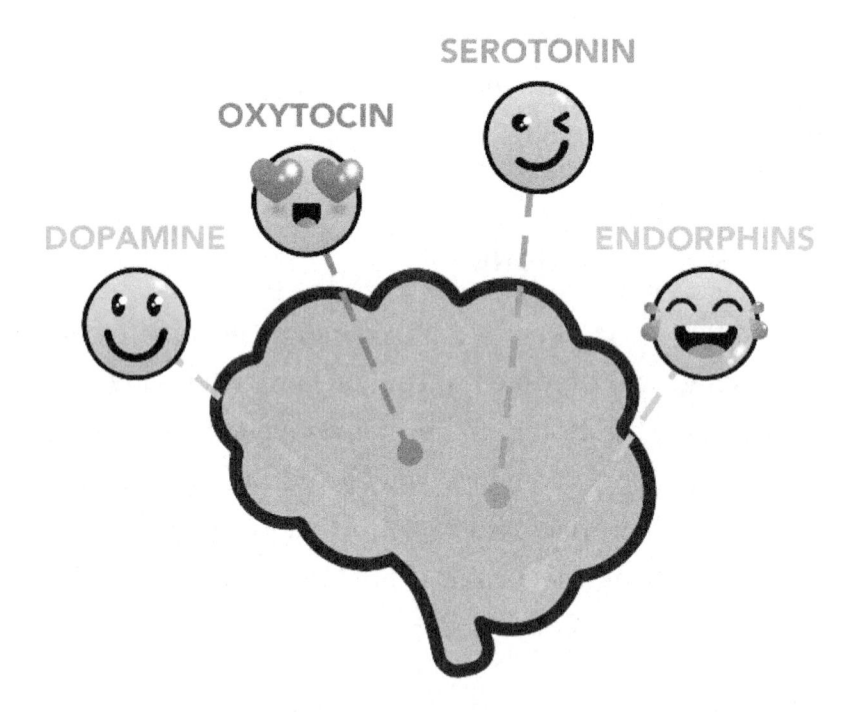

Participants often find themselves giggling uncontrollably, and by the end of a session, the room is filled with contagious, positive energy. (Check out my 5minTEDx talk at this link: https://www.youtube.com/watch?v=auysQyvYsS0.) Laughter yoga is a reminder that humor doesn't always need a punchline. Sometimes, just the act of laughing is enough to lift your spirits and wash away stress. You can even fake it till you make it, as the body doesn't know the difference between a real laugh and a pretend laugh!

Funny mishaps are bound to happen when you're in the thick of caregiving. These moments, while frustrating at the time, often become cherished memories, stories that bring a smile to your face long after the fact. Embracing humor means allowing yourself to see the lighter side of life, to chuckle at the unexpected twists and turns that caregiving throws your way. It's about finding joy in the little things, even when they don't go according to plan.

Incorporating humor into your daily life doesn't require grand gestures. It can be as simple as watching a comedy show after a long day or listening to a humorous podcast while running errands. Sharing jokes and funny stories with friends can also lighten the mental load, creating moments of connection and camaraderie. It's about weaving laughter into the fabric of your routine, allowing it to become a source of strength and resilience.

The benefits of laughter extend beyond the immediate joy it brings. Scientifically speaking, laughter triggers the release of endorphins, those feel-good chemicals that act as natural stress busters. It reduces stress hormones and increases blood flow, promoting both physical and mental well-being.

It's like a mini-workout for your brain, leaving you more relaxed and at ease.

Laughter can even reset your vagus nerve, a crucial part of your body's stress management system. One of my books, "Young Hearts Wise Souls," delves into how this works, offering insights and tips on how you can harness the power of laughter to cultivate a sense of calm. So, next time you find yourself amid a caregiving whirlwind, remember to pause and let out a good laugh. It's not just a way to cope; it's a tool for healing, a reminder that even in the busiest of days, there's always room for a bit of joy.

REAL-LIFE EXAMPLES: TURNING POINTS AND TRIUMPHS

Let's meet Emma, who was at a crossroads when a career change collided with her caregiving responsibilities. Emma was an accomplished marketing executive, climbing the corporate ladder with high heels and a killer instinct for closing deals. But when her father was diagnosed with Alzheimer's, she had to rethink her priorities.

The thought of stepping back from a career she loved was daunting, to say the least. Yet, within this challenge, Emma discovered an unexpected opportunity. She transitioned into a part-time role, allowing her to dedicate more time to caregiving. At first, the shift felt like a loss, but soon, she realized that this change offered her something invaluable: the chance to redefine success on her terms.

Emma discovered a passion for writing, pouring her experiences into a blog that connected her with a community of caregivers. This pivot didn't just change her career path; it transformed how she viewed herself and her place in the world.

Perspective is a powerful thing. Take Ben, for instance. Ben initially saw caregiving as a series of hurdles, a new challenge to conquer each day. However, a conversation with a fellow caregiver inspired him to view his role differently. Instead of focusing on the difficulties, Ben began to embrace the joy hidden within the small moments—a shared laugh with his grandmother, the satisfaction of helping her find comfort in an otherwise difficult day.

This shift in perspective didn't erase the challenges, but it added a layer of richness and meaning to his experience. Ben found unexpected joy and fulfillment in his role, realizing that caregiving was about managing tasks, nurturing relationships, and creating memories.

Resilience often lies in how we react to the unexpected. Consider Anna, who faced an unforeseen challenge when her husband's health took a sudden turn. The weight of new responsibilities threatened to overwhelm her, but Anna chose to adopt a positive outlook. She focused on what she could control, seeking resources and support that empowered her to manage the situation.

By embracing a proactive approach, Anna discovered her own strength and resilience. She tackled each new day with determination and grace, turning potential setbacks into steppingstones. Her story is a demonstration of the transformative power of resilience, showing that even the most demanding challenges can become growth opportunities with the right mindset.

Now it's your turn to seek out those pivotal moments. Reflect on your own caregiving experiences and consider the turning points that have shaped your path. What challenges have you faced, and how have they influenced your perspective? Identify personal growth moments where you discovered new strengths or developed skills you didn't know you had. Create a space to explore these reflections, whether through journaling, art, or conversation.

Remember, these moments are not just markers of change but opportunities to embrace your evolving story and find empowerment in your unique journey. Caregiving is not a static role—it's a dynamic, ever-changing experience with the potential for profound personal transformation. Embrace it, and let your story unfold.

As we close the chapter on shifting perspectives, remember that your view shapes your reality. By

embracing change and seeking growth, you can transform challenges into opportunities.

3

BUILDING EMOTIONAL RESILIENCE

Imagine you're at a grand buffet, each dish representing an emotion. You've got happiness pastries, sadness stews, and a big bowl of frustration fondue. Now, instead of piling your plate high with a chaotic mix, you learn to pick and choose, savoring each flavor for what it is.

Welcome to the world of emotional intelligence—a fancy term for the art of understanding and managing your emotional buffet. Emotional intelligence, or emotional quotient (EQ), is like having a GPS for your emotions. It helps you navigate the tumultuous terrain of caregiving with grace and composure, ensuring you don't get lost in the sauce.

At its core, emotional intelligence is a set of skills that can transform your caregiving experience. It consists of four main components: self-awareness, self-regulation, social awareness, and relationship management.

Picture self-awareness as a mirror that reflects your emotions, allowing you to recognize and understand them without judgment. It's that moment when you realize your frustration isn't just about spilled milk but maybe the accumulation of stress from the day.

Self-regulation is the pause button on your emotional remote control, helping you manage your responses in caregiving situations. It's the ability to take a deep breath instead of snapping when your loved one asks the same question for the fifth time. You'll read all about how I learned to be with Mom and her constant repetitions about her childhood soon.

Social awareness is like having an emotional radar, enabling you to tune into the feelings of others. It's the skill that helps you notice when your care recipient is having a tough day, even if they haven't said a word.

Finally, relationship management is about orchestrating harmonious interactions. It's the glue that holds your relationships together, allowing you to navigate conflicts with family members and communicate effectively with those in your care. Together, these components form the backbone of emotional intelligence, providing you with the tools to handle the emotional rollercoaster that is caregiving.

So, why is emotional intelligence such a big deal for caregivers? For starters, it enhances communication with care recipients. When you're in tune with your emotions, you're better equipped to express your needs and understand theirs. It's like switching from a fuzzy AM radio to a crystal-clear FM station, where everyone hears and understands the broadcast.

This clarity reduces misunderstandings and fosters stronger connections, making caregiving a collaborative journey rather than a solo expedition. Moreover, emotional intelligence improves conflict resolution with family members. Instead of letting disagreements escalate into family feuds, you can address issues calmly and constructively, fostering an environment of cooperation and support. Once again, I recognize this is not easy.

Developing emotional intelligence is like learning to play an instrument. It requires practice, patience, and a willingness to hit a few wrong notes along the way. One effective strategy is journaling, which can help increase self-awareness. As previously discussed, you record your emotional landscape by writing down your thoughts and feelings, allowing you to identify patterns and triggers. It's like having a backstage pass to your emotional concert, where you can see what's happening behind the scenes. Over time, this practice can enhance your ability to recognize and manage your emotions, making you a more empathetic and responsive caregiver.

To cultivate emotional intelligence, start by setting aside a few minutes each day for self-reflection. Consider questions like, "What emotions did I experience today?" and "How did I respond to challenging situations?" This introspection can reveal valuable insights, helping you fine-tune your emotional radar.

Additionally, practice active listening during interactions with your loved one. Focus on their words, tone, and body language, allowing yourself to pick up on subtle cues that might otherwise go unnoticed. This attentiveness fosters empathy and strengthens your relationships, turning caregiving into a partnership built on understanding and trust.

Incorporating these strategies into your daily routine can transform how you approach caregiving. Emotional intelligence is more than just a skill set; it's a superpower that equips you to handle the complexities of caregiving with resilience and compassion.

Whether navigating a difficult conversation or simply sharing a quiet moment with your loved one, your emotional intelligence will guide you, ensuring that your caregiving journey is one of connection and growth. So, grab your emotional compass and embark on building emotional resilience. After all, in the grand buffet of life, it's not just about what you put on your plate, but how you savor each bite.

MINDFUL BREATHING: A DAILY PRACTICE OF SELF-AWARENESS

Picture yourself in the middle of a chaotic day, your mind racing faster than a caffeinated squirrel. You've got deadlines at work, a doctor's appointment to remember, and a loved one who needs your attention. It feels like you're juggling flaming swords while riding bareback on a horse.

But what if you could pause the whirlwind for just a moment and find a pocket of calm amidst the storm? Enter mindful breathing, your new best friend in stress reduction. This simple practice is like hitting the reset button on your internal chaos, allowing you to step back and breathe—literally.

Mindful or conscious breathing is all about focusing your attention on the breath, a natural rhythm that often goes unnoticed in the hustle of daily life. Directing your focus to each inhale and exhale creates a mental oasis, a space where the mind can find peace and clarity. It's like switching from a blaring rock concert to a tranquil symphony, where every note soothes the soul.

As you breathe mindfully, you'll notice the tension in your shoulders start to melt away, your mind shifting from frantic to focused. It's like putting on noise-canceling headphones in a crowded airport—everything around you remains the same, but your perception changes, bringing a sense of calm.

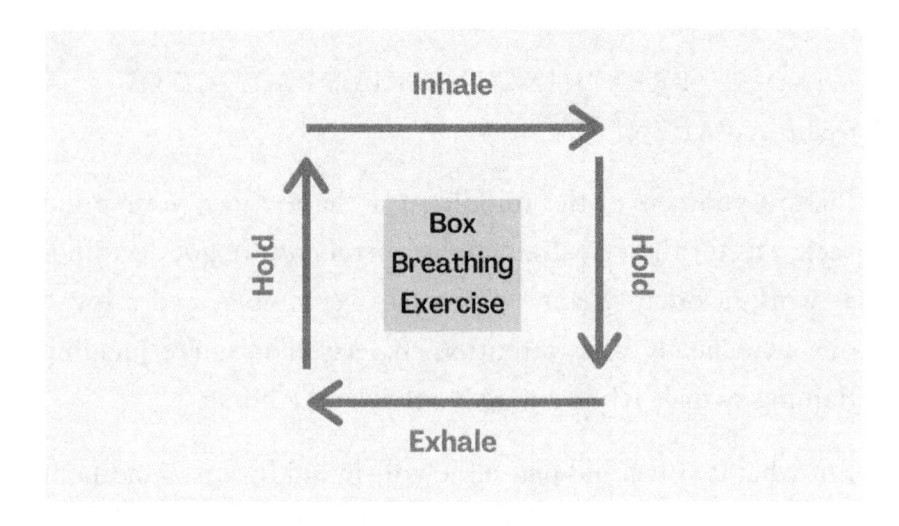

```
        Inhale
   ┌─────────────>┐
   │              │
   │   ┌─────┐    │
Hold│   │ Box │    │Hold
   │   │Breathing│  │
   │   │Exercise│  │
   │   └─────┘    │
   │              ▼
   └<─────────────┘
        Exhale
```

To get started with mindful breathing, let's walk through a couple of basic techniques. The first is diaphragmatic breathing, also known as belly breathing. Find a comfortable position, either sitting or lying down. Place one hand on your chest and the other on your belly. Inhale deeply through your nose, allowing your diaphragm to expand and your belly to rise. Feel the air fill your lungs, then exhale slowly through your mouth, letting your belly fall. Repeat this cycle a few times, focusing on the rise and fall of your breath. It's like a gentle wave, washing over you and carrying stress away with the tide.

Another technique to try for its quick stress-relief effects is box breathing. Imagine drawing a square with your breath. Inhale for a count of four, hold for four, exhale for four, and hold again for four. Repeat this pattern, visualizing each side of a box as you breathe. The structured rhythm can help ground you, providing a sense of stability and control when everything else feels like it's spinning out of orbit. It's the perfect tool to keep in your back pocket for those moments when the world seems overwhelming.

The benefits of mindful breathing extend beyond the immediate sense of calm. Regular practice can lower blood pressure, reduce heart rate, and even improve digestion. It's like giving your body a mini-spa-day without needing fluffy robes or cucumber slices. Mentally, mindful breathing cultivates clarity and focus, helping you navigate the complexities of caregiving with a steady hand. As you incorporate conscious breathing into your routine, the noise of daily stress fades to a whisper, and a newfound sense of peace occurs.

As my Mom's carer, I discovered that a few minutes of mindful breathing each day helped me find emotional balance amidst the demands of caregiving. It became my secret weapon, a way to recharge and face each day with renewed strength. Whether in the car, at my desk, or preparing dinner, I found moments to practice mindful breathing, transforming my caregiving experience from a burden to a source of connection and joy.

To make mindful breathing a regular part of your life, consider setting reminders for breathing breaks throughout the day. If you've been in one of my audiences, you would have received a tiny little pink sticker to remind you. Pair these breaks with daily activities like commuting or waiting in line, turning mundane moments into opportunities for mindfulness. It's like adding a sprinkle of Zen to your routine, infusing each day with a touch of tranquility. As you embrace mindful breathing, you'll discover that peace is not a distant destination, but a state of being you can cultivate, one breath at a time.

COMPASSION FATIGUE: ACKNOWLEDGING AND OVERCOMING

Imagine you've been on a rollercoaster all day—looping through emotional highs and lows without a seatbelt. That's a glimpse into compassion fatigue, often lurking in the shadows of caregiving. It's like a slow leak in your emotional tire, where empathy drips out until there's not much left to give. Think of it as empathy fatigue, where the well of understanding and patience starts to run dry.

Unlike burnout, which feels like hitting a wall, compassion fatigue is more of an erosion. It creeps in as emotional and physical exhaustion from the relentless act of caring, leaving you feeling like a deflated balloon at the end of a child's birthday party.

Recognizing compassion fatigue in yourself can be tricky. You might feel detached or apathetic toward those you care for. The once-vibrant empathy that colored your caregiving world fades into a gray landscape of indifference. Your patience wears thin, and irritability becomes the unwelcome guest who overstays. Frustration bubbles up over the most minor things—a misplaced key, a forgotten appointment—and you wonder where your usual calm has gone. This emotional withdrawal can be disconcerting, leaving you questioning your capability and commitment as a caregiver.

So, what's the antidote to this emotional fatigue? It's time to roll up your sleeves and dive into the toolbox of self-support. Regular self-support activities are like giving your emotional engine a much-needed tune-up. Start by carving out time for activities that replenish your spirit, whether a walk in the park, a cup of tea enjoyed without interruption, or a creative hobby that brings you joy.

Self-support is not an indulgence; it's a necessity, like keeping your phone charged during a power outage. Yes, you know exactly how that feels when your cell phone is showing low battery and you race for the charger. And let's not forget the importance of seeking professional support. Sometimes you need an outside perspective to help you navigate the emotional maze. Therapy or counseling can offer a safe space to process your feelings, providing coping strategies for compassion fatigue.

Take, for example, the story of a nurse named Lisa, who found herself drowning in the demands of her job. She was the go-to person for her colleagues, always ready with a smile and a helping hand. But over time, the weight of her responsibilities became overwhelming. Feeling detached and exhausted, Lisa sought help through therapy and discovered the power of peer support.

By sharing her experiences with fellow caregivers, she found solace and understanding. Therapy equipped her with tools to manage her emotions. At the same time, her support group reminded her that she wasn't alone in her struggles. Lisa regained her compassion and energy through these connections, transforming her caregiving experience from a draining chore to a fulfilling endeavor.

Stories like Lisa's remind us that compassion fatigue, while challenging, is not insurmountable. It's a call to action, a reminder to prioritize your own well-being as much as you do for those you care for. By acknowledging the signs and taking proactive steps, you can replenish your emotional reserves and regain the joy that caregiving brings.

It's about finding balance, like a tightrope walker steadying themselves with each step. Remember, your ability to care for others is directly linked to how well you care for yourself. So, embrace self-support as a vital part of your routine, and let it guide you back to the vibrant, compassionate caregiver you know you can be.

TRANSFORMATIVE POWER OF SELF-COMPASSION

Picture this: you're at the end of a long day, the kind where everything that could go wrong did. The laundry's still in the washer, the dog chewed up your favorite slippers, and your loved one spilled tea over the freshly cleaned floor. It's tempting to let frustration take over, beat yourself up over not being the perfect caregiver, or mutter curses about how nothing ever goes as planned.

But what if you decided to be your best friend instead of being your harshest critic? That's the essence of self-compassion—treating yourself with the same kindness and understanding that you'd offer a dear friend. It's about acknowledging that, yes, life can be a chaotic mess and you're doing the best you can in the storm. Self-compassion is the gentle voice that says, "Hey, it's okay. You're human, and you're enough."

The importance of self-compassion for caregivers cannot be overstated. Self-compassion is your anchor in the relentless dance of caretaking, where emotions can swing from joy to frustration faster than a seesaw. It's being gentle with yourself, especially when faced with failures or setbacks. This kindness fosters an environment where you can grow emotionally, becoming more flexible and resilient.

Instead of getting bogged down by guilt or self-criticism, self-compassion helps you bounce back (or forward) like a rubber band snapping back into shape after being stretched. It turns the narrative from "I can't believe I messed up again" to "It's okay to make mistakes; it's how I learn."

Now, how do you cultivate this magical self-compassion? Enter loving-kindness meditation, a practice where you focus on sending goodwill and kindness to yourself and others. Find a quiet corner, close your eyes, and imagine a warm light surrounding you, filling you with peace. Silently repeat phrases like, "May I be happy. May I be healthy. May I be safe." Feel the warmth of those words, letting them wash over you.

Dr. Kristen Neff, a pioneer in self-compassion research, also suggests incorporating mindfulness and common humanity into your routine. Mindfulness helps you stay present, acknowledging your feelings without judgment, while common humanity reminds you that everyone struggles—you're not alone in this. (I'll come back to mindfulness in chapter 4.)

Self-reflective journaling, mentioned earlier, is a powerful tool here too. It's like having a heart-to-heart with yourself on paper. Write about your day, the highs and lows, and explore how you felt. Instead of critiquing yourself, approach these reflections with curiosity and kindness. Ask yourself, "What did I learn from today?" or "How can I be kinder to myself next time?" This exercise boosts self-awareness and strengthens your ability to respond to challenges with compassion.

Take Phillip, a caregiver who transformed his self-talk and, ultimately, his well-being. He used to criticize himself relentlessly, caught in a loop of guilt and self-doubt. However, through daily self-compassion practices, Phillip learned to treat himself with the same warmth he extended to his loved one. He would remind himself that it was okay to have an "off" day and that perfection was never the goal. Over time,

Phillip noticed a shift. He felt lighter, more resilient. His mental health improved, and he approached caregiving with renewed energy and optimism.

Phillip's story is a reflection of the power of self-compassion. It's not about eliminating mistakes or erasing challenges, but about meeting them with a gentle heart. So, the next time you're tempted to harshly judge yourself for a misstep, pause. Take a deep breath, and remember that you deserve the same kindness you so freely give to others.

EXERCISES FOR EMOTIONAL RESILIENCE

Imagine preparing for a storm—not the kind that rattles your windows with thunder, but the emotional squalls that caregiving often brings. Building emotional resilience is like constructing a sturdy shelter that keeps you grounded even when the winds of stress howl. One way to fortify this emotional shelter is through visualization techniques.

Picture a peaceful place, perhaps a serene beach or a tranquil forest. My go-to picture is when I once laid on my back in a river and a pelican flew overhead. Close your eyes and immerse yourself in your mental landscape. Hear the waves gently lapping at the shore or the leaves rustling in the gentle breeze. Visualization provides a mental escape hatch, allowing you to step away from stress, if only for a moment. It's like a mental vacation without the need for sunscreen or bug spray.

Another tool in your resilience toolkit is cognitive reframing. This technique involves shifting your perspective, much like adjusting the lens on a camera to bring a blurry image into focus. When faced with a challenging situation, pause and ask yourself, "Is there another way to view this?" Perhaps your loved one's insistence on wearing mismatched socks is less a fashion faux pas and more an exercise in creative expression.

Reframing helps transform obstacles into opportunities, turning roadblocks into steppingstones. It encourages flexibility in thought, allowing you to navigate caregiving's twists and turns with a bit more grace and a little more humor.

Repetition is the key to resilience-building. Like any skill worth having, emotional resilience thrives on regular practice. Set aside a few minutes each day for these exercises, whether during your morning coffee or as a bedtime ritual. Think of it as a daily workout for your mind, strengthening your emotional muscles to better handle whatever comes your way. As you cultivate this routine, you'll find that the resilience you build spills over into other areas of your life, enhancing your ability to cope with stress at work, home, and everywhere in between.

Community also plays a starring role in bolstering emotional strength. Take the story of James, a caregiver who faced a health crisis head-on and emerged with newfound resilience. When his wife's condition took a sudden downturn, James initially felt overwhelmed, like he was drowning in a sea of responsibilities. But by committing to daily resilience exercises and leaning on his support group, he discovered a strength he never knew he had.

Visualization helped him find calm amidst the chaos, while cognitive reframing allowed him to approach challenges with creativity and hope. James's journey is evidence of the power of resilience, a reminder that even in the darkest moments, there's a light waiting to be discovered.

In the grand tapestry of caregiving, resilience is the thread that binds us together. It's the ability to bounce forward, to face adversity with courage, and to find joy in the everyday moments. As you weave these resilience-building practices into your life, you'll find that stress becomes less of an adversary and more of a dance partner, one you can twirl with grace and maybe even a few fancy footwork moves. So, gather your tools, embrace the journey, and remember that resilience isn't just about weathering the storm—it's about learning to dance in the rain.

4

PRACTICAL SELF-SUPPORT STRATEGIES

Imagine you're a superhero, cape fluttering in the breeze, ready to save the day. But there's a twist—you're juggling a dozen responsibilities while trying to rescue the metaphorical cat stuck in a tree. Welcome to the paradox of caregiving, where you're expected to perform superhuman feats while balancing the never-ending to-do list. Although hopefully by now you have your own "get-to-do" list.

Before you whip out your invisible lasso to rope in more hours, let me introduce you to a secret weapon that's a game-changer for caregivers: time blocking. This nifty tool is like giving your day a makeover, transforming chaos into a symphony of organization and calm. It's about carving out time for yourself, finally making self-support a non-negotiable part of your routine. I first introduced this into my life in 2001 when my boyfriend (now husband) Mark suggested I schedule in some "white space" into my calendar. And all these years later there is still white space for me in there!

Time blocking is your trusty sidekick in this superhero saga. Think of it as a structured plan, assigning specific time slots for different tasks, including the ever-elusive self-support. It's like creating a weekly playlist, each block of time dedicated to a particular tune, bringing harmony to your day.

Start by creating a time block calendar, a visual map guiding you through the labyrinth of daily duties. Allocate blocks for everything from caregiving responsibilities to work tasks and, most importantly, self-support. Yes, you read that right—self-support gets its own dedicated block. It's not an optional extra; it's essential, like oxygen for your well-being.

Setting boundaries around these personal non-negotiable time blocks is crucial. Picture them as your fortress of solitude, a sacred space amidst the hustle, where interruptions are as welcome as a mosquito at a picnic. Communicate these boundaries with your family and friends, letting them know that you're off the clock during these times, recharging your batteries. It's your time to unwind, reflect, and prepare for the day ahead, free from the demands of caregiving or the incessant ping of notifications.

Scheduling self-support is like planting seeds in a garden; it requires regular attention to flourish. Make self-support as much of a priority as your caregiving tasks. Just as you wouldn't skip a loved one's medical appointment, don't skip your self-support time. By prioritizing yourself, you're not being selfish; you're ensuring you have the energy to care for others. It's the classic oxygen mask analogy—put yours on first to better assist those around you.

Now, let's talk about how to structure these precious self-support blocks. Start your day with a morning routine that includes time for reflection and preparation. Whether it's a few minutes of stretching, sipping your favorite brew, or journaling, these moments set the tone for a balanced day. In the evening, wind down with relaxation rituals—anything from reading a good book to enjoying a warm bath. And hey, if there's no time for a bath right now, I'll share my nightly routine. Lavender spray on my pillow, lip balm, and hand cream. That's it. These routines bookend your day with peace, helping you transition smoothly from the demands of caregiving to moments of tranquility.

Staying consistent with time blocking can be challenging. But with a few strategies, you can maintain this practice. Use alarms or reminders to stay on schedule, like a gentle nudge from your virtual assistant, ensuring you don't skip your self-support slots. Regularly review and adjust your time blocks as needed. Life as a caregiver is dynamic, and flexibility is key. If a block isn't working, tweak it. The goal is to create a rhythm that works for you, a dance where you lead, not the day's demands.

Interactive Element: Time Block Template

Try creating your own time block calendar. Grab a planner or use a digital tool like Google Calendar. Start by color-coding different tasks, with a unique hue for self-support. As you fill in your schedule, remember to include breaks and downtime. This visual tool will help you see where your time goes and ensure self-support gets the spotlight it deserves.

PERSONALIZED SELF-SUPPORT ROUTINES

So, you've decided to embrace self-support—hooray! It's not just about bubble baths and chocolate (though delightful); it's about creating a routine that truly fits you, like a favorite pair of fuzzy slippers. The key to unlocking this wellness treasure trove is to tailor your self-support practices to your unique needs and preferences.

Start by taking a step back and assessing what you really need. Perhaps you're someone who recharges by spending time alone, or maybe you're a social butterfly who gains energy from being around others. Think about the activities that bring you joy and relaxation. Is it the quiet solitude of a good book (maybe even this one), or the exhilarating rush of a morning jog? Identifying what uniquely works for you is like finding the golden ticket to your health and happiness.

Personalized self-support routines aren't just nice to have; they're game-changers when it comes to stress relief and overall well-being. When you engage in activities that resonate with you, motivation skyrockets. Instead of dragging your feet to a generic spin class that everyone swears by, you'll look forward to your chosen activities.

This increased motivation leads to greater satisfaction and a genuine sense of fulfillment. It's like finally discovering that perfect coffee blend that makes mornings bearable. Plus, when self-support is tailored to you, it's much more effective at stopping stress in its tracks, transforming you from a frazzled mess into a Zen master. Well ... almost.

Let's dive into some simple ways to recharge that you might really enjoy!

If you've got a creative streak, why not try painting or writing? Let your imagination run wild on a canvas or pour your thoughts onto paper. For those who find solace in physical activity, swimming or yoga can provide a perfect outlet for tension. Feel the stress melt away as you glide through water or stretch into a downward dog.

And don't underestimate the power of social engagements. Spending time with supportive friends, sharing laughs and stories, can uplift your spirits and remind you that you're not alone in this caregiving gig.

Flexibility and adaptability are your best friends when maintaining a self-support routine. Life is unpredictable, especially when juggling caregiving and a full-time job. Be open to adjusting your activities as your needs change. Maybe that outdoor run you loved in the summer needs to shift to indoor yoga during the winter months. Or perhaps you've developed a newfound interest in pottery after a spontaneous class with a friend. Embrace these changes and welcome new hobbies into your life. Your self-support routine isn't set in stone; it's a living, breathing thing that evolves with you.

As you embark on this self-support adventure, remember it's all about you. There's no one-size-fits-all approach, and what works for someone else might not work for you—and that's perfectly okay. This is your chance to create a routine that supports your well-being, nurtures your soul, and brings a smile to your face. So explore, experiment, and find what truly lights you up. Your personalized self-support routine reflects your individuality and what a unique and wonderful person you are.

MINDFUL MOMENTS: INTEGRATING MINDFULNESS INTO BUSY DAYS

Picture this: you're in the middle of a hectic day, juggling tasks like a circus performer with too many balls in the air. The phone rings, emails ping, and the laundry pile seems to be multiplying like rabbits. Letting the chaos sweep you away is tempting, but what if you could pause, even for a moment, and find a pocket of peace amidst the storm? Enter mindfulness, your new ally in tranquility. Mindfulness isn't about dedicating hours to meditation or becoming a Zen master overnight. Instead, it's about finding brief moments of presence throughout your day, transforming the mundane into the extraordinary.

Start with mindful eating during mealtimes. Instead of scarfing down your lunch like it's a race, take a moment to appreciate each mouthful. Notice the flavors and textures, the way the food feels as you chew. It's like turning a rushed pit stop into a gourmet experience. You can also practice mindful listening in conversations with loved ones. When your partner or child speaks, can you give them your full attention? Put down the phone, look them in the eye, and really hear what they're saying. This simple act can deepen your connections, turning everyday chats into meaningful exchanges.

The beauty of micro-mindfulness practices lies in their simplicity. These brief moments of awareness can significantly reduce stress and anxiety, like a mental massage for your busy brain. Mindfulness helps clear the fog, increasing your focus and clarity, so you can tackle the day with renewed energy. It's like cleaning your mental windshield, giving you a clear view of the road ahead. The mental health benefits are substantial, offering a buffer against the whirlwind of daily life and helping you maintain your equilibrium.

There are countless ways to incorporate mindfulness into your routine. Try practicing gratitude while commuting. Instead of grumbling about the traffic or crowded train, take a moment to appreciate the opportunity to pause and reflect.

Notice the world around you—the trees swaying in the breeze, the clouds floating lazily by. Or, during short breaks at work, take a mindful walk. Feel the ground beneath your feet, the air on your skin, the rhythm of your breath. These moments of connection with the present can transform the ordinary into the extraordinary, offering a much-needed respite in your day.

To keep mindfulness at the forefront of your mind, you can use your phone alarm here too. Set your phone alarm to prompt you for mindful pauses, like a tender reminder from the universe to slow down and breathe. Visual cues, like sticky notes with encouraging messages, can also serve as reminders to engage in mindfulness. Place them where you'll see them often—on your computer monitor, the bathroom mirror, or the refrigerator door. These cues are a loving reminder to pause, breathe, and reconnect with the present moment.

Integrating mindfulness into your day doesn't require a complete lifestyle change. It's about weaving these small, intentional practices into your routine, allowing them to ground you amidst the chaos. These mindful moments are like steppingstones, guiding you through the tumultuous waters of caregiving with grace and ease. So, next time you find yourself swept away by the whirlwind of responsibilities, remember that peace is just a breath away. Mindfulness transforms even the busiest day into a tapestry of calm, connection, and clarity.

DIGITAL DETOX: RECLAIMING YOUR PEACE OF MIND

Imagine your brain as a hamster on a wheel, running 24/7 thanks to the endless notifications, emails, and social media updates pinging away like a relentless game of whack-a-mole. It's enough to make anyone want to throw their phone out the window and return to carrier pigeons. But before you do anything drastic, let's talk about a digital detox—the practice of unplugging from technology to reclaim some much-needed peace of mind.

In today's hyper-connected world, setting boundaries for screen time isn't just a suggestion; it's a lifeline. Establishing tech-free zones in your home can transform your environment into a sanctuary, where digital noise is muted and simplicity reigns supreme. Picture your kitchen table as a haven for conversation, or your bedroom as a retreat for rest. These zones act as buffers between you and the digital world, offering a break from the constant barrage of information that can lead to burnout.

It's no secret that constant connectivity can wreak havoc on caregivers. The persistent buzz of devices pulls your attention in a thousand directions, leaving you feeling like a circus performer juggling flaming torches. This digital overload can increase feelings of anxiety as your brain struggles to keep up with the relentless pace. It's the equivalent of trying to read a book while someone shouts random trivia in your ear.

The distraction becomes a companion, sapping your ability to focus and leaving you frazzled. And let's not forget the impact on sleep. The blue light emitted by screens tricks your brain into thinking it's still high noon, making it difficult to wind down and catch those critical Zs. It's like having a disco ball in your bedroom, minus the groovy music.

So, how do you escape this digital hamster wheel? The answer lies in scheduling regular digital detox days. Think of them as minivacations for your mind, a chance to disconnect and recharge. On these days, resist the urge to check your devices, and instead, immerse yourself in offline activities. Dive into a book gathering dust on your shelf, or get your hands dirty in the garden. Feel the earth between your fingers, and let nature work its magic. These activities offer a grounding effect, pulling you back into the tangible world where life's simple pleasures reside.

Real-life stories illuminate the transformative power of a digital detox. Take Emily, a caregiver who was caught in the digital whirlwind. Her phone was her constant companion, a source of stress she didn't even realize existed. After implementing a digital detox, Emily found her mental clarity and focus improved dramatically. She described it as lifting a fog that had dulled her senses and muddled her thoughts. With the digital noise quieted, Emily could reconnect with her surroundings, appreciating the beauty in everyday moments she previously missed. Her story shows what can happen when you step back and unplug.

Digital detoxing isn't about abandoning technology altogether. It's about reclaiming control, setting boundaries, and finding balance in a world that often demands more than we can give. In these quiet moments away from screens, you'll discover a sense of peace that's been waiting patiently beneath the surface. Once a frenetic battlefield, your mind becomes a tranquil garden, a place where creativity and calm can flourish. So go ahead, embrace the detox, and let your spirit breathe without the weight of the digital world pressing down on you.

QUICK WINS: 10-MINUTE SELF-SUPPORT SOLUTIONS

Picture this: you're in the middle of a hectic day, and every minute feels like it's slipping away faster than sand through an hourglass. Yet, amidst the chaos, there's a little oasis waiting for you—quick self-support wins. These are the micro self-support practices you can sprinkle throughout your day, offering brief but effective moments of relief. It's like finding spare change behind your couch cushions: small, but surprisingly satisfying. These ten-minute treasures are perfect for when your schedule is tighter than your favorite pair of jeans after the holidays.

This is the perfect time to include some of the breathing exercises we discussed earlier. Or perhaps try this short exercise. Find a quiet spot, close your eyes, and inhale deeply through your nose, then exhale slowly through your mouth. Feel your shoulders drop as the tension melts away. It's another mini-vacation for your mind, no passport required. Or you might try quick stretches to relieve that pesky tension. Stand up, reach for the sky, and feel the satisfying pop of your spine. It's like hitting the refresh button on your body, giving you a burst of energy to tackle the next task.

Let's explore a few more ten-minute self-support gems. How about listening to your favorite song and dancing like no one's watching? Close the door, hit play, and let the music move you. It's fun, it's freeing, and it's a calorie-burning workout all in one. Or perhaps enjoy a cup of tea while practicing deep breathing. As you sip, take slow, intentional breaths, and let the warmth seep into your soul. It's a moment of tranquility that grounds you amidst the whirlwind.

Or take the opportunity to jot down some thoughts in your gratitude journal, helping to shift your focus from stress to gratitude. The beauty of these quick wins lies in their cumulative effect. Like drops of water filling a bucket, each small action adds up over time, creating a reservoir of well-being.

By incorporating these micro-practices into your day, you're building a self-support habit. It becomes second nature, like brushing your teeth or checking if the milk's gone bad before pouring it into your cereal bowl. Over time, these small efforts significantly improve your overall well-being, reducing stress and enhancing your mental clarity.

Encourage yourself to find your own quick wins. Experiment with different self-support practices and see what resonates with you. A five-minute meditation app may be your go-to (one-minute is fine too!), or a quick doodle session might unlock your creativity. There's no right or wrong way to do it; it's all about discovering what brings you joy and relaxation. My own lightbulb moment came with the simple act of applying some hand cream. There was something unexpectedly soothing about taking a moment to massage the cream into my hands, breathing in the calming scent. It was a small act of care that made me feel more centered and ready to face whatever the day threw my way.

Incorporating these quick wins doesn't require you to overhaul your life. It's about finding those little pockets of time and using them to recharge. These moments of self-support are like tiny gifts you give yourself, reminding you that amidst the demands of caregiving, you matter too. So embrace these quick wins, and watch as they transform the rhythm of your day, one small step at a time.

5

SETTING BOUNDARIES WITHOUT GUILT

Imagine you're a superhero in a world where your superpower is saying yes to everything. But instead of saving the day, you're drowning in a sea of obligations, with an endless to-do list. Sound familiar? Welcome to the life of a caregiver! It's easy to feel like a perpetually overworked superhero, trying to juggle caregiving, work, and a semblance of a social life without losing your mind. But here's the secret no one tells you: the real superpower is learning to say no without guilt.

Saying no is crucial for safeguarding your personal well-being and preventing that dreaded burnout from sneaking up on you like a stealthy ninja. Prioritizing self-support over additional commitments is not a self-indulgence—it's essential.

You need to recognize your personal limits and capacity to ensure you're not stretching yourself thinner than a pancake on a hot griddle.

It's about knowing when to tap out and recharge your batteries so you can continue being the fantastic caregiver you are without turning into a frazzled, stressed-out version of yourself.

Now, let's dive into some practical **scripts** for saying no without sounding heartless. Picture this: your boss asks you to take on an extra project at work, but your plate is already overflowing. You could say, "Thank you for considering me for this project. However, I'm currently at capacity and couldn't give it the attention it deserves." Or imagine a friend inviting you to a last-minute dinner party, but you were planning on a quiet night in. Try, "I appreciate the invite, but I've had a long week and need some downtime to recharge. Let's catch up soon, though!"

Let's paint a few scenarios where saying no becomes a superpower. Picture a friend calling you in a panic, asking for last-minute help with moving. You're tempted to drop everything and help, but you remember your boundaries. You say, "I'm sorry, I can't help this time, but I hope the move goes smoothly!" I can hear that little voice inside your head already telling you that this can't be done and you must help your friend.

Or consider a family member requesting extra caregiving duties when you're already stretched thin. You respond, "I'd love to help, but I'm already committed to my current responsibilities. Perhaps we can explore other options together?" These scenarios highlight the importance of practicing your "no" responses beforehand, so you're prepared when the situation arises.

Of course, saying no often comes with a side dish of guilt. But here's the thing: refusing additional demands is an act of **self-respect**, not selfishness. It's about affirming the importance of your personal needs and understanding that you can't pour from an empty cup. When you're overwhelmed, you can't be the caregiver you aspire to be. So, **reframing** your refusal as a necessary step in maintaining your well-being can help manage the guilt that often accompanies it.

When those pangs of guilt creep in, remind yourself that saying no is a way to set healthy boundaries, allowing you to be more present and effective in the commitments you choose to say yes to. It's about making intentional choices that align with your values and priorities, rather than getting swept away by the currents of obligation and expectation. Embrace the power of no as a tool for self-support and balance, and watch as it transforms your world, one decision at a time.

Interactive Element: Practice Saying No

Take a moment to think about recent situations where you wish you had said no. Grab a journal or paper, and write down those scenarios. Then, craft a polite yet firm response for each one, using the examples above as inspiration. Practice saying them out loud, in front of a mirror or with a supportive friend. This exercise will help you feel more confident in setting boundaries and prioritizing your needs. Remember, it's okay to put yourself first sometimes—even superheroes need a break!

BOUNDARY SETTING WITH FAMILY AND FRIENDS

Imagine a world where everyone magically understands your needs without you ever having to say a word. Sounds like a dream, right? Unfortunately, that's not how real life works. In the whirlwind of caregiving, setting boundaries with family and friends is like drawing a line in the sand to protect your own oasis of sanity.

Without clear boundaries, you risk drowning in a sea of resentment and burnout. It's like trying to fill a bucket with a hole in the bottom—no matter how much you pour in, it never seems enough. When you clearly communicate your personal needs and limits, you're preserving your well-being and nurturing healthier relationships. It's about finding that delicate balance where your needs are respected and your relationships thrive on mutual understanding.

Setting boundaries might sound daunting, but with some planning, you can navigate these conversations like a pro. Begin by choosing the right time and setting. You don't want to bring up boundary discussions during a chaotic family dinner (trust me, I learned this the hard way) or when everyone's rushing out the door.

Find a quiet moment when you can have a calm, uninterrupted conversation. This isn't a monologue, so prepare to listen as much as you speak. Use "I" statements to express your feelings and needs, which helps prevent the other person from feeling attacked. For example, instead of saying, "You never help me," try, "I feel overwhelmed when I don't have support." It's a subtle shift but opens the door to dialogue rather than defensiveness.

Of course, setting boundaries isn't as simple as flipping a switch. You might encounter resistance or pushback from others, especially if they're used to you being the go-to person for every need and whim. It's like teaching an old dog new tricks—it takes time and patience. (Refer back to those mindfulness exercises to train your patience.)

When faced with resistance, stay firm yet compassionate. Remind your loved ones that setting boundaries ensures you can remain there for them in the long run. Consistency is key. Maintaining boundaries over time requires being like a gardener tending to delicate plants. If you neglect them, those boundaries might wither, leading to confusion and frustration.

Let me share a story about a caregiver named Leonie who faced this challenge. Leonie was the glue that held her family together, always ready to drop everything immediately when others wanted her help. But the constant demands took a toll on her mental health. One day, she decided enough was enough.

She sat down with her family and explained how overwhelmed she felt. Her voice trembled, but she pressed on, using "I" statements to communicate her needs. At first, her family was taken aback. They hadn't realized the impact their expectations had on her. However, over time, as Leonie consistently upheld her boundaries, something extraordinary happened. Family dynamics improved, and everyone learned to respect her limits. Leonie's story is indication of the power of clear communication. It's a reminder that you have a voice that deserves to be heard.

BALANCING WORK AND CAREGIVING RESPONSIBILITIES

Imagine you've got one foot in the office and the other at home, both demanding your attention like a pair of squabbling siblings. You're not just a caregiver but also a full-time employee, trying to juggle deadlines, meetings, and a mountain of emails. It's like playing a game of Twister where every spin adds another layer of complexity.

The stressors pile up, creating a weight that feels like you're carrying a backpack full of bricks. You're expected to perform at your peak in both roles, with time and energy stretched thinner than your patience on a Monday morning. The demands never seem to let up, and you constantly shift gears, trying to keep everything from crashing down.

Finding balance might feel like searching for a needle in a haystack, but it's not impossible. Time management is your trusty steed in this quest for equilibrium, like the time block strategy from chapter 4.

I touched on delegation earlier, and it's another superhero skill that can lighten your load. Don't hesitate to pass tasks to colleagues when your plate is overflowing. It's not about shirking responsibilities; it's about teamwork and efficiency. At home, involve family members in caregiving duties. Whether cooking dinner, helping with errands, or managing appointments, sharing the load prevents burnout. Think of it as a team sport where everyone plays a role in keeping things running smoothly.

Open communication with your employer is crucial. If the thought of broaching the topic makes you break out in a cold sweat, take a deep breath. Begin by requesting a meeting to discuss your current responsibilities and how they impact your caregiving role. At this juncture, it's beneficial to discuss with your manager the ways in which your caregiving responsibilities might influence your performance and mood at work too.

Many workplaces offer flexible options like remote work or adjusted hours. Don't be afraid to ask for what you need. Lay out your case clearly, focusing on how these changes will enhance your productivity and well-being. Set clear expectations around your availability, ensuring that work and caregiving commitments don't clash like titans battling for supremacy.

Success stories abound, illustrating how others have mastered the balancing act. Take Jamie, a financial analyst who was in the thick of managing projects and caring for his elderly father. The constant back and forth was taking its toll. By negotiating a remote work arrangement, Jamie found the flexibility he needed to excel in both roles.

He set up a home office with a comfortable chair and a potted plant for company. The ability to work from home allowed him to handle caregiving emergencies without the stress of commuting. Jamie's story affirms the power of clear communication and proactive problem-solving.

Another caregiver, Beth, contacted her company's employee assistance program for support. She discovered resources and counseling services that provided a lifeline when the demands felt overwhelming. By tapping into these offerings, Beth gained insights into managing stress and maintaining a healthy work-life balance. Her once-chaotic days transformed into a more manageable rhythm, where work and caregiving coexisted harmoniously. These examples highlight the importance of utilizing available resources, whether workplace programs or community support.

Balancing work and caregiving is a dynamic dance that requires constant adjustment and adaptability. It's about finding that sweet spot where responsibilities align rather than collide. So, embrace the tools and strategies at your disposal, and remember you're not alone in this balancing act. Through innovative thinking and steadfast resolve, you can adeptly manage the complexities of balancing these two demanding roles.

PROTECTING YOUR PERSONAL TIME

Imagine your personal time as a rare, exquisite bird that, if not carefully protected, might fly away, never to be seen again. Personal time is vital for caregivers, a lifeline that keeps you tethered to your sanity. It's not just about sitting in a quiet room, though that sounds dreamy; it's about the opportunity to relax and rejuvenate, much like a quick power nap that leaves you feeling brand new.

Dedicating time to yourself helps reduce stress, a silent saboteur that creeps up and leads to burnout faster than an internet outage ruins movie night. It's a necessity, not a nicety, for maintaining mental and physical health. Personal time allows you to recharge your batteries, so you can face the world—or at least the laundry pile—with renewed energy.

Now, you might be thinking, "Easier said than done!" But safeguarding your personal time is doable with a few practical strategies. The first step is to schedule regular personal days or hours. Consider these mini-vacations, even if they're just spent in your favorite armchair with a good book.

It's about creating a routine where you prioritize yourself without apology. Communicate the importance of this time to those around you. A simple "I'll be offline for an hour" or "I'm taking Sunday afternoons for myself" sets a clear expectation that this time is sacred. Let others know that during these periods, you're unavailable, like a celebrity in a spa retreat.

Certainly, maintaining personal time can often seem as challenging as steering a ship through a storm—daunting, yet not insurmountable. One of the most significant barriers is the sneaky, nagging feeling of guilt or selfishness accompanying self-support. You might worry that taking time for yourself is neglecting your duties, but it's quite the opposite.

When you're well-rested and refreshed, you're better equipped to handle the demands of caregiving. To overcome this guilt, remind yourself that personal time is an investment in your well-being and, by extension, in the care you provide. Handling interruptions or emergencies is another hurdle. Life happens, and sometimes your personal time gets hijacked. When that occurs, try to reschedule your downtime as soon as possible, treating it with the same importance as any other commitment.

Let's peek into the life of Jack, a dedicated caregiver who learned the value of reclaiming personal time. Jack was running himself ragged, constantly on call for his family and never taking a moment for himself. Realizing he was on the brink of burnout, Jack established a weekly "me time" ritual.

Every Saturday morning, Jack would head to the local park, leave his phone behind, and go for a long walk. This ritual became his reset button, a time to clear his mind and enjoy the simple pleasure of nature. Over time, he found that this small act of self-support had a profound impact on his well-being. As I've been saying all along, it's the little things that can often have the biggest impact. Jack returned to his caregiving duties with a clearer mind and more patience, proving that a little personal time can go a long way.

In wrapping up this chapter, consider setting boundaries and protecting your personal time as laying the foundation for a more balanced and fulfilling life. By carving out these sacred moments for yourself and respecting them as you would any other obligation, you ensure that you're surviving and thriving. As we transition into the next chapter, remember that these small steps lead you toward a healthier, happier you.

MAKE A DIFFERENCE WITH YOUR REVIEW

UNLOCK THE POWER OF KINDNESS

"No act of kindness, no matter how small, is ever wasted."

— AESOP

Have you ever felt like your stress is taking over? Like no matter how much you do, there's always more waiting? That's burnout—and it's pretty tough. But guess what? You're not alone.

The Burnout Blueprint was created by me to help busy people—just like you—find simple ways to stress less, set healthy boundaries, and feel better, without feeling guilty about it. And your words could help someone else find the same relief.

Most people pick books after reading reviews. Your review could help:

- one more parent feel calmer at home.
- one more worker enjoy their job again.
- one more teacher find balance.
- one more friend feel happier.
- one more person just like you, feel less alone.

Leaving a review takes just a minute and costs nothing, but it could change someone's whole day.

Ready to spread kindness and help someone beat burnout?

Simply scan the QR code below and leave your review:

Thank you for making a difference!

6

ENHANCING RELATIONSHIPS

Imagine you're in a sitcom where every episode revolves around a quirky family mishap. There's laughter, maybe a little chaos, and always a heartfelt moment that ties everything together. Now picture your life as a caregiver—a bit like that sitcom, except sometimes it feels like you're doing it all without a script. Relationships, especially with loved ones, form the backbone of this show. They can be both the comic relief and the dramatic tension. But, unlike TV magic, real-life relationships require effort, honesty, and a sprinkle of vulnerability to thrive, especially when caregiving is involved.

COMMUNICATING NEEDS: OPENING UP TO LOVED ONES

Open communication acts as the foundation for any solid relationship. It's like the Wi-Fi signal that keeps everything connected. Without it, misunderstandings and miscommunications start to pile up like unread emails.

To keep things running smoothly, sharing your needs and feelings with the people in your life is crucial. This transparency reduces those pesky miscommunications and fosters a supportive environment where everyone feels heard and valued. Imagine expressing your needs without feeling like you're speaking in riddles. By communicating openly, you create a space where both you and your loved ones can thrive.

Sharing your needs effectively involves a few tried-and-true techniques, just like the "I" statements I shared with you earlier. It shifts the focus from blame to expressing how you feel, making it easier for your loved one to understand your perspective. Many people find this revolutionary in their relationships—including me!

Timing is also key. Choose a moment when both of you are calm and receptive, not in the middle of a heated debate or when you're balancing a precarious tower of laundry. Find a quiet space, maybe over a coffee or during a walk, where you can speak freely and listen actively.

Vulnerability can feel like standing on stage in your pajamas, but it's essential to building trust. It's easy to worry that opening up will burden others or cause conflict. Yet sharing gradually can help ease these fears. Start small, like dipping your toes in before diving into the deep end. Share a little, gauge the response, and build from there. This gradual approach strengthens trust and makes opening up less daunting. Remember, it's not about unloading everything at once but about creating a dialogue where both parties feel comfortable sharing.

Take, for instance, the story of Alex, a caregiver who transformed his marriage by communicating his stressors. Initially, Alex bottled everything up, believing he had to be the stoic pillar of strength. But this approach left him feeling isolated and frustrated. One evening, over dinner, he decided to share his feelings with his spouse, discussing his struggles and how they affected him. To his surprise, his openness was met with understanding and support.

Together, they worked on a plan to balance caregiving responsibilities, strengthening their relationship and making it more resilient. This open dialogue alleviated Alex's stress and deepened their connection, proving that sharing truly is caring.

Interactive Element: Reflective Journaling Prompt

Take a moment to reflect on your own communication with your loved ones.

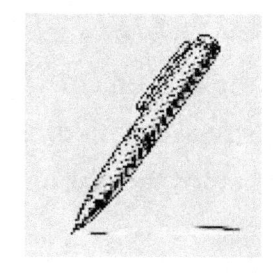

Consider a recent conversation where you felt misunderstood or where your needs weren't met. What could you have said differently? Write about how you might use "I" statements to express your feelings in a future conversation. This practice can help you articulate your thoughts more clearly and create a roadmap for more effective communication.

QUALITY TIME: MAKING THE MOST OF MOMENTS TOGETHER

Time—it's the one thing we're all short on, especially when juggling caregiving, work, and the hundred other things on your list. But here's the kicker: It's not how much time you spend with loved ones that counts, but how you spend it. Ever notice how a meaningful moment can stick with you longer than an entire day spent together? That's the magic of quality over quantity. Those shared experiences, the ones where you truly connect, create lasting memories. They build a bridge between hearts, even when life's responsibilities pull you in different directions.

The emotional connections you make aren't just about putting in the hours. They're about the depth of interaction, the shared laughter, and the understanding in a glance. In these moments, fleeting yet profound, relationships grow stronger, building a foundation of love and trust that withstands the test of time.

So, how do you maximize this quality time? Start by penciling in regular date nights or family activities, just like you would a dentist appointment or a team meeting. These planned moments are like little oases in the desert of daily life. Whether it's a quiet dinner at home, a board game night, or a weekend outing, these activities create space for connection.

Consider engaging in shared hobbies or interests, like cooking, gardening, or even tackling a DIY project. Doing something together, where both parties are invested, turns simple tasks into bonding opportunities. And hey, if you're both terrible at painting but decide to try anyway, the laughter over your abstract masterpieces will be a memory to cherish.

Presence and mindfulness play pivotal roles in enhancing these interactions. Imagine sitting with a loved one, but instead of listening, your mind's wandering to tomorrow's to-do list. Being present means giving your undivided attention and actively listening without the constant urge to check your phone.

My own experience with my mom taught me the gift of listening. Sometimes, she just needed to talk, well … actually to repeat herself over and over as she deteriorated, and all I had to do was be there, fully. Mindfulness helps you appreciate these moments, grounding you in the now, and allowing the richness of the interaction to unfold. It's like finding a hidden gem in a sea of pebbles.

My lasting memory of Mom is us making pastry together and her hands on the rolling pin with me. She had no idea of my name and that I was her daughter but she vividly remembered making pastry with her own mother. This memory still brings me so much joy.

If you need ideas, think about cooking a meal together. It's not just about the food; it's the shared experience of chopping vegetables, tasting sauces, and maybe even a flour fight or two. Or try taking a scenic walk or hike with a partner. Nature offers a backdrop for conversation, reflection, or even comfortable silence. These activities don't require grand gestures or elaborate planning. They're simple yet meaningful ways to connect, reminding us that sometimes the best moments are the ones spent together, without the distractions of daily life.

MANAGING EMPATHY OVERLOAD

Imagine you're at a smorgasbord, not of food, but of emotions, where your tray is piled high with everyone else's feelings. Welcome to empathy overload, where the lines blur between your emotions and those of others.

As a caregiver, your empathy is often on overdrive, leading to emotional exhaustion and strain on your relationships. When you're constantly tuned into the care recipient's emotions, separating your feelings from theirs becomes challenging. You carry the weight of the world's worries, like a one-person band trying to play every instrument simultaneously.

This blurring of emotional boundaries reduces your availability for your other loved ones and leaves little energy for your own needs. You might feel like a battery running on low, unable to recharge because you're too busy powering everyone else's flashlight. It's no wonder that empathy overload can leave you feeling more drained than a cell phone with too many apps running in the background.

To manage this empathetic flood, setting emotional boundaries becomes a lifeline. Think of it as creating a protective bubble or shield around yourself, where you can choose which emotions to let in and which to keep at bay. It's not about closing yourself off but preserving your energy for when it truly matters. Self-reflection can help you identify which emotions are yours and which belong to someone else. Take a moment each day to check in with yourself and ask, "How do I feel?" This simple question can act like a compass, guiding you back to your emotional center. When you recognize your feelings, it becomes easier to manage them, ensuring you're not overwhelmed by external influences.

Emotional self-regulation is another crucial tool in navigating empathy overload. It's like having a thermostat for your emotions, allowing you to adjust them before they reach boiling point. Techniques for calming emotional responses can be as simple as deep breathing or a quick walk around the block.

A great piece of advice was given to me when I was looking after Dad. "If it gets too heated, tell him you're just leaving the room to wash your hands." I would then go and do that a little more slowly than normal and when I got back, often Dad had forgotten what we were talking about. The hand-washing was a regular reset for me. These small acts serve as mental resets, helping you regain control and approach situations clearly.

Recognizing triggers that send your emotions spiraling is also key. Once you're aware of these triggers, you can take proactive steps to manage them—whether setting limits on how much news you consume or taking breaks from emotionally intense conversations.

Consider the story of Suzie, a caregiver who felt like a sponge soaking up everyone's emotions. At one point, she realized she was more familiar with her neighbor's drama than her own feelings. By incorporating mindfulness into her routine, she learned to observe emotions without getting swept away. Mindfulness offered her a new perspective, allowing her to acknowledge feelings without judgment and decide which ones to engage with.

Suzie's story is a great example of the power of balancing empathy with self-support. She found that by setting boundaries and practicing mindfulness, she could be present for others without losing herself in the process.

Managing empathy overload isn't about shutting out the world but finding a healthy balance. It's about being there for others while also being there for yourself. So, the next time you feel like your emotional cup runneth over, remember that it's okay to take a step back, breathe, and refill your own cup first. After all, you can't pour from an empty one. And, over time, you could even be able to fill your cup whilst pouring for others. Wouldn't that be a great goal to aspire to?

REBUILDING CONNECTIONS: REPAIRING STRAINED RELATIONSHIPS

Imagine juggling while riding a unicycle on a tightrope. That's caregiving for you, and while it might sound like a circus act, it's the reality for many of us. This high-wire act can strain personal relationships to the breaking point. The constant demands of caregiving create increased tension, leading to misunderstandings that crop up faster than dandelions in spring. You might find that the time you once spent nurturing relationships is now consumed by the endless list of caregiving tasks. Neglect of relationship maintenance isn't intentional, but it happens, like forgetting to water a plant until it wilts. The bonds that once felt unbreakable start to fray, and the emotional distance grows until it feels like an unbridgeable chasm.

But fear not! Rebuilding these connections is possible, turning that chasm into a bridge stronger than ever. It starts with honest discussions about past grievances. Think of it as spring cleaning for your emotions, dusting off old grudges and airing them out.

These conversations aren't easy, but they're necessary. Approach them with an open heart and a willingness to listen. Sit down with your loved ones and share your feelings, acknowledging where things went off course. This dialogue isn't about assigning blame but understanding each other's perspectives.

By facing these issues head-on, you create a foundation for healing. Once the air is cleared, focus on creating shared goals for the future. What do you both want to achieve in this relationship? Whether spending more time together or supporting each other's dreams, having common goals brings you closer, like two climbers scaling a mountain side by side.

Forgiveness and acceptance are the linchpins in this process. Holding on to past conflicts is like carrying a backpack full of rocks—weighing you down. Practicing forgiveness rituals or exercises can help lighten this load, freeing you to move forward.

Consider writing a letter to yourself, acknowledging the hurt, and then letting it go. It's a symbolic act, like releasing a balloon into the sky and watching it float away. Acceptance, too, plays a vital role. Accepting imperfections in oneself and others means recognizing that nobody's perfect, and that's okay. It's about embracing the quirky, sometimes messy reality of relationships and finding beauty in the imperfection. It's like loving a handmade quilt for its unique, uneven stitches.

Take the story of Mark and David, siblings who found themselves at odds while caring for their aging mother. The stress of juggling responsibilities led to arguments and a growing distance between them. But instead of letting their relationship wither, they chose to come together for an honest conversation. They aired their grievances, acknowledged their stress, and decided to work as a team.

Together, they created a plan to share caregiving duties, allowing each of them time for rest and personal pursuits. Through forgiveness and acceptance, they rebuilt their bond, stronger and more resilient than before. Their joint efforts in caregiving strengthened their relationship and enriched their lives, bringing them closer as brothers and friends.

Rebuilding connections isn't always easy, but it's worth the effort. It's about turning challenges into opportunities for growth, like a phoenix rising from the ashes. As caregivers, you already know the value of resilience. By applying that same determination to your relationships, you can repair what's been strained, creating connections that support and sustain you through the ups and downs of caregiving.

BUILDING A SUPPORT NETWORK: LEANING ON OTHERS

Ever feel like you're the lead in a one-person show without an understudy in sight? That's caregiver life for you. All the responsibility, none of the backup. It's easy to become isolated, your world shrinking to the size of your to-do list.

But here's the plot twist: you don't have to do it alone. Enter the support network, your cast of characters ready to help you carry the load. Having a network isn't just a nice-to-have; it's crucial. It's the difference between feeling like a lone island and being part of a bustling archipelago.

A strong support system can reduce the isolation and feelings of being overwhelmed that often accompany caregiving. It provides practical assistance, like running errands or offering childcare, and emotional support when the going gets tough. Think of it as your pit crew, ensuring you're fueled and ready to keep racing.

Building this network isn't about sending out bat signals or smoke signals—though feel free to try these if you think they'll work. Start by identifying the people around you who can offer support. Friends, family, even neighbors can be invaluable resources.

Sometimes, people want to help but don't know how. So, take the plunge and reach out. You might be surprised at how willing they are to lend a hand, whether helping with a home repair or just listening over a cup of coffee. Beyond your immediate circle, explore community resources.

Many localities offer caregiver support groups or online communities where you can connect with others who understand your challenges. These groups can become a lifeline, providing advice, encouragement, and the occasional reality check. Joining a support group is like finding your tribe—people who get it, no explanations needed.

Reciprocity is the glue that holds support networks together. It's not just about receiving help; it's about giving back when you can. Sharing resources, like an excellent meal delivery service or a fantastic podcast, can help others in your network. Offering your time or expertise in return, even in small ways, strengthens these bonds. It creates a cycle of support, where everyone benefits. You become part of a community that uplifts each other, like a row of dominoes standing strong, ready to catch the one that wobbles. This balance of give-and-take ensures that your network remains robust and resilient, able to weather the ups and downs of caregiving.

Take the story of Jane, a caregiver who discovered the power of community through her local support group. Initially hesitant to join, Jane was embraced by a diverse group of caregivers, each with unique stories and struggles. Together, they shared challenges and triumphs, forming a circle of trust and understanding.

Jane marveled at the relief from knowing she wasn't alone, that others had walked similar paths and emerged stronger. The camaraderie she experienced lifted her spirits, providing a safe haven where she could be herself. This support network didn't just help Jane manage caregiving; it enriched her life, reminding her of the strength found in unity.

As we wrap up this chapter on enhancing relationships, remember that connections are the heartbeat of caregiving. They're your support, your allies, your lifeline. Whether leaning on others, sharing your journey, or finding strength in community, relationships are where the magic happens. They remind you that you're never truly alone even on the most challenging days.

7

TOOLS FOR LONG-TERM SUCCESS —WITH ANYTHING!

Imagine you're about to embark on a grand adventure. Your rucksack is packed with all the essentials: snacks, a map, and maybe even a trusty compass. But wait a minute—what about that invisible tool we often overlook? That's right, I'm talking about self-efficacy. This secret sauce boosts confidence and competence in all areas of life, especially when you're knee-deep in the rollercoaster world of caregiving.

Albert Bandura, a psychological guru, introduced this gem of a concept, and it's all about believing in your ability to manage and succeed in specific situations. It's my top topic when I talk at keynotes all over the world, and I call it your INNER MBA. People say to me "But I thought you talked about burnout?" "Yes," I say, "I do. But I talk about the missing piece of burnout that nobody really talks about."

Think of self-efficacy as your internal cheerleader, whispering sweet encouragements like, "You've got this!" even when you're elbow-deep in chaos. It's the key to unlocking potential, tackling obstacles, and transforming challenges into mere steppingstones.

Self-efficacy plays a crucial role in caregiving because, to be honest, the job often feels like attempting to solve a Rubik's Cube blindfolded. The endless to-do lists and emotional demands make it easy to feel overwhelmed. But with self-efficacy in your toolkit, you can navigate these hurdles with the grace of a cat landing on its feet. It's not just about caregiving, though.

High self-efficacy spills over into every nook and cranny of life, making you a pro at handling whatever curveballs life throws your way. Whether you're negotiating a tricky work situation or trying to convince your toddler that broccoli is, in fact, the superior vegetable, self-efficacy gives you the edge.

I've broken down Bandura's four-step model into three, just because it's easier to remember things in threes, which many people call the Rule of Three. Your Inner MBA is your blueprint for boosting that self-efficacy meter.

YOUR INNER MBA

First up, **M**astery experiences. It's all about building confidence through successful caregiving tasks. Imagine the satisfaction of changing a flat tire for the first time. Each successful caregiving task, no matter how small, adds a brick to your wall of confidence.

Then are your efficacy **B**uilders, through vicarious experiences and social persuasion. You can learn vicariously by observing other caregivers. It's like watching a cooking show and realizing you can whip up a soufflé without setting the kitchen on fire. Seeing others succeed helps you believe you can too. And I've coupled this with social persuasion, where positive feedback and encouragement from others can be the wind beneath your wings. It's that moment when someone says, "You're doing a great job," and suddenly you feel like you could conquer the world.

Finally, emotional and physiological states, or **A**wareness as I like to call it. Managing your emotional responses to stress is like mastering the art of Zen, even when the world feels like it's spinning faster than a top.

Let's put these steps into action with some real-life scenarios. Start by setting small, achievable caregiving goals, like organizing a week's worth of medication or scheduling a fun activity for your loved one. No matter how modest, each accomplishment boosts your confidence and reinforces your self-efficacy. Consider joining caregiver workshops or support groups to learn from peers. It's like adding tools to your belt, each equipping you for the journey ahead. You'll find yourself inspired by others' success stories, ready to tackle your challenges with newfound vigor.

As your self-efficacy grows, so too will your resilience and well-being. You'll find yourself approaching caregiving responsibilities with greater confidence, like a seasoned captain navigating familiar waters. Problem-solving becomes second nature, and you'll tackle caregiving situations with the finesse of a master chess player. It's about building that internal reservoir of strength that allows you to face each day with a smile, even when the road is rocky. So, embrace the power of self-efficacy—your steadfast companion in caregiving and beyond.

WEATHERING THE STORM: STRATEGIES FOR SUSTAINED RESILIENCE

Picture this: you're in the middle of a torrential downpour, metaphorically speaking, where caregiving duties, work obligations, and life's curveballs all rain down at once. Now, you could stand there getting soaked, or you could whip out an umbrella called resilience. Resilience is your ability to withstand adversity without losing your mind or sense of humor.

Developing a proactive approach to problem-solving is one of the key spokes in this umbrella. Instead of waiting for challenges to snowball into crises, tackle them head-on. It's like playing chess with life, always thinking a few moves ahead. Identify potential stressors and craft a plan of action. It's not about having all the answers, but about being ready to find them.

Cultivating optimism is another vital spoke. It's like having a flashlight in the dark, guiding you with a positive outlook even when things seem bleak. Optimism doesn't mean ignoring the storm; it means believing there's a rainbow on the other side.

Now, let's peek into the toolbox of stress management and recovery techniques. Deep relaxation techniques are like a cozy blanket for your mind, helping to untangle the tension knots.

Consider practices like progressive muscle relaxation, where you tense and then release each muscle group, or guided imagery, which transports you to a peaceful place in your mind. It's like taking a mental vacation, minus the sandy toes. Engaging in restorative activities, like a leisurely stroll through a nature, can also work wonders. Nature has this magical ability to soothe the soul and clear the mental fog. Breathing in fresh air and feeling the sun on your face is like hitting the refresh button on your brain.

Let's not forget the magic of routine and consistency. Think of a structured routine as the foundation of a sturdy house, providing stability when life gets shaky. Establishing daily caregiving rituals creates a sense of predictability, reducing stress and enhancing efficiency.

Whether it's a morning routine that sets a positive tone or an evening ritual that winds down the day, consistency is your ally. Balancing work, caregiving, and leisure time is a bit like juggling flaming torches, but with the right routine, you'll find a rhythm that works. It's all about creating harmony, where each part of your day flows seamlessly into the next, giving you the space to breathe.

Take a page from the playbook of resilient caregivers who've weathered their fair share of storms. Meet Clara, a caregiver who faced a health crisis that would've knocked the wind out of anyone's sails. But Clara leaned into her resilience strategies like a sailor in a tempest, gracefully steering her ship.

She approached each challenge with a calm determination, breaking down daunting tasks into manageable pieces.

Clara also tapped into her community, drawing strength from those around her. Her proactive problem-solving and unwavering optimism saw her through, emerging stronger on the other side. Clara's story recognizes the power of resilience, a reminder that even the fiercest storms can be weathered with the right mindset and tools.

Resilience isn't about never falling; it's about getting back up, dusting off, bouncing forward and facing the next wave with a determined grin. By incorporating these strategies into your daily life, you'll find that resilience becomes more than just a concept—it becomes a way of life, empowering you to tackle each challenge with confidence and courage.

ADAPTING TO CHANGE: EMBRACING FLEXIBILITY

Caregiving is like trying to nail jelly to a wall—something shifts when you think you've figured it out. You're not alone in this topsy-turvy ride. Adaptability is not just a nifty skill; it's the backbone of surviving and thriving in caregiving. The needs of those you care for can change faster than the weather.

Everything's smooth sailing one day; the next, you're navigating a sea of unexpected medical visits and medication changes. New environments or circumstances can pop up seemingly out of nowhere, like surprise party guests who forgot to RSVP. Being open to these changes isn't about having all the answers. It's about being willing to roll with the punches and reinvent the game plan when necessary.

To cultivate flexibility, start with mindfulness. It's about staying present and aware, even when the world feels like it's doing a cha-cha around you. Simple mindfulness exercises can help you stay grounded, allowing you to respond rather than react to changes. Picture yourself as a tree, rooted but swaying with the wind—strong, yet flexible.

Then there's creative problem-solving, like having a Swiss Army Knife for your brain. Challenge yourself with puzzles or brain teasers, activities that keep your thinking sharp and adaptable. This mental agility will prepare you to tackle caregiving challenges with a fresh perspective and a can-do attitude.

Innovation plays a starring role in caregiving. It's about trying new techniques or technologies, like introducing a tablet to help your loved one stay connected with family through video calls. You could explore alternative solutions, like setting up a care schedule that involves friends and family and provides you with a break from the daily grind.

Embracing technology doesn't mean you're turning into a robot caregiver, although apparently they do exist out there too! It's about using the tools available to make life a tad easier. Imagine the time saved with automated medication reminders or apps that track medical appointments and health records. It's not just about efficiency; it's about giving you peace of mind and more time to focus on what truly matters.

Take the story of Jake, a caregiver who had to adapt when his family relocated abruptly. Suddenly, he found himself caring for his mother remotely, a challenge that initially seemed insurmountable. But Jake embraced the change, setting up video calls for daily check-ins and employing a local caregiver to assist with in-person tasks. He used technology to monitor her medication and health updates, ensuring he was always in the loop.

Jake's story illustrates the power of adaptability and innovation, showing that even when faced with what seems like an impossible situation, there's always a path forward with a bit of creativity and a willingness to embrace change.

Adaptability in caregiving isn't just about survival; it's about finding joy in the unexpected, like discovering a new favorite song when you hit shuffle. It's about keeping an open mind and a flexible spirit, ready to embrace whatever comes your way with a smile and a dash of humor.

CREATING A RESILIENCE TOOLKIT

Imagine you're a carpenter with a toolbox full of gadgets, each one designed to tackle a specific problem. Now, swap out the hammers and nails for tools that enhance your resilience in caregiving. A resilience toolkit is precisely that

—a collection of resources and strategies tailored to support your personal strength and adaptability. Think of it as your go-to survival kit for navigating the peaks and valleys of caregiving.

Your toolkit should be as unique as you are, reflecting your needs, preferences, and the challenges you face. Start by identifying the tools that resonate with you, whether a calming playlist that lifts your spirits or a series of uplifting quotes that remind you of your inner strength. Inspirational books can be compelling, offering words of wisdom and motivation when the going gets tough. Consider titles that speak to resilience, self-support, and mindfulness, turning to them like old friends when you need a boost.

Stress-relief tools are another vital component of your resilience toolkit. Picture yourself squeezing a stress ball during a tense moment, feeling the tension ebb away with each squeeze. Or perhaps fidget toys are more your speed, providing a tactile way to release nervous energy. These small, unassuming tools might seem trivial, but they can make a world of difference when you're feeling overwhelmed. They act as tiny pressure valves, helping manage stress before it boils.

Customization is key, so include items that bring you comfort and joy, whether a favorite snack, a scented candle, or a photo of a cherished memory. These personal touches transform your toolkit into a sanctuary, a portable oasis you can turn to whenever you need a moment of peace.

Keeping your resilience toolkit up-to-date is like maintaining a well-loved garden. Regular attention and occasional pruning are required to ensure it remains at its best. Periodically review the items in your toolkit, asking yourself if they continue to serve you well. Many of the people I've met in the past couple of years have remembered about things that worked in the past ... you know, BC (before Covid).

Maybe that book you once found so inspiring no longer resonates, or perhaps you've discovered a new podcast that leaves you feeling rejuvenated. Swap out old tools for new ones that better align with your current needs, ensuring your toolkit evolves as you do. This ongoing refinement process keeps your toolkit fresh and relevant, ready to support you through whatever challenges come your way.

Consider the story of Karen, a caregiver who found solace and strength through her well-curated resilience toolkit. Karen's toolkit included a collection of poetry that spoke to her soul, a meditation app that provided moments of calm, and a gratitude journal where she documented daily blessings.

During particularly challenging periods, Karen turned to her toolkit, finding comfort in the familiar tools she had carefully chosen. The poetry reminded her of the beauty in the world, even amidst chaos. At the same time, the meditation app offered a chance to reset and recharge. Her gratitude journal became a record of her resilience, filled with reminders of small victories and moments of joy.

Karen's experience highlights the transformative power of a thoughtfully assembled toolkit, a sign of the strength that lies within when we take the time to nurture and support ourselves.

REAL-LIFE STORIES: RESILIENT CAREGIVERS

Imagine waking up each day to what feels like a new episode of a never-ending drama series, where each scene is improvised and the plot twists are relentless. This is the daily reality for many caregivers, yet incredible tales of resilience lie within these stories of unpredictability.

Take Mia, for example, who found herself caring for her husband after a debilitating accident. Overnight, her world shifted from sharing responsibilities to shouldering them alone. But Mia wasn't one to back down. She approached each day with determination, crafting a new normal from the pieces of their former life. Her story is one of perseverance, of learning new skills and finding strength in every small victory, like the first time her husband smiled after weeks of silence.

Then there's Raj, a devoted son caring for his mother with Alzheimer's. It's a role that can feel like grasping at sand, filled with moments of profound connection and equally deep loss. Raj found solace in building a strong support network. Friends, family, and a local caregiver group became his pillars, offering advice, shared experiences, and sometimes just a listening ear when the days felt too heavy. Raj's story highlights the power of community and the resilience that comes from knowing you're not alone in the trenches.

What do these resilient caregivers have in common? A shared theme of perseverance runs through their narratives. They face each challenge head-on, refusing to be defined by adversity. Instead, they adapt and find creative solutions, often turning obstacles into opportunities for growth. Determination is their compass, guiding them through the fog of uncertainty. Strong support networks are another common thread. These caregivers lean on their communities, drawing strength from the bonds of shared experience and understanding. It's a reminder that resilience isn't a solo act; it's a choir, harmonizing the voices of those who walk the same path.

These real-life examples serve as both inspiration and a gentle nudge to reflect on your own journey. Consider the resilience milestones you've reached. It could be navigating a difficult medical appointment or finding a moment of laughter in a sea of stress. Each milestone is a strength, a badge of honor earned through grit and grace.

Journaling can be a powerful tool for capturing these achievements. Reflect on the challenges you've faced and the resilience you've cultivated. Write about a time you felt overwhelmed and how you overcame it. What did you learn about yourself in the process? How did it shape your perspective? These reflections honor your journey and reinforce your resilience, reminding you of the well of strength within.

Like Mia and Raj, resilient caregivers transform their caregiving experience by embracing resilience as a mindset. It's not about having all the answers but about finding the courage to keep going, even when the road is steep. Their stories encourage us to see challenges not as insurmountable mountains but as steppingstones, each one bringing us closer to a fuller, richer life.

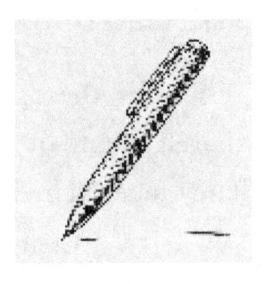

Resilience is about finding light in the darkest moments, about growing through what you go through. As you continue your caregiver journey, remember that resilience is not a destination but a way of being. Draw strength from these stories, and let them guide you as you navigate the ever-changing caregiving landscape.

8

MANAGING EMOTIONAL STRESS

Imagine waking up each day feeling like you've been hit by a truck, only to remember you didn't actually leave your bed. It's not a physical ailment but emotional exhaustion that has parked itself in your life without an invitation. This isn't just about being tired—it's about feeling like every cell in your body is waving a little white flag.

Emotional exhaustion is a frequent flyer for caregivers, boarding the plane with emotional baggage heavier than any suitcase. It sneaks up on you, like that last slice of pie you didn't need, but somehow, you ate anyway. Emotional exhaustion is a state where you're depleted, mentally and physically, like a cell phone battery perpetually stuck at 1%. And yet we always race for the charger when our phone battery is low! What about your own battery? It affects your ability to function, making even the simplest tasks feel like climbing Everest in flip-flops (or "thongs" as we say over in Australia).

The symptoms are as pesky as a mosquito in your bedroom at midnight. You're fatigued, not just from lack of sleep, but from carrying the emotional weight of caregiving. It's a tiredness that seeps into your bones, wrapping you in a heavy blanket of lethargy. Irritability becomes your new sidekick, snapping at the slightest provocations. And then there's the sense of helplessness, a feeling that no matter how much you do, it's never enough. This trifecta of symptoms creates a perfect storm, leaving you stranded in an overwhelming sea.

So, what brings on this emotional exhaustion? Picture a never-ending conveyor belt of demands, each more urgent than the last. Caregiving is a full-time gig that doesn't clock out at 5pm. It's a relentless cycle of emotional labor, where your heartstrings are constantly tugged in different directions. Constantly neglecting rest and relaxation is like endlessly swimming against the current. Even when you do manage to sneak in a nap, it's often interrupted by the call of duty. The emotional demands from care recipients add another layer to the exhaustion, as you're constantly navigating their needs and emotions, often at your own expense.

But fear not, for there are ways to combat this emotional fatigue and reclaim your energy. It starts with the basics—

regular rest and relaxation activities. I know, I know, rest sounds like a mythical creature, but even small pockets of downtime can make a world of difference. Whether it's a 15-minute meditation session, a leisurely walk in the park, or simply sitting in silence with a cup of tea, these moments of pause allow you to recharge.

Engaging in hobbies that bring joy is another powerful antidote. Think of it as a mini-vacation for your brain, a chance to disconnect from caregiving and reconnect with yourself. Whether painting, gardening, or knitting a sweater for your cat, these activities provide a sense of accomplishment and joy.

SEEKING HELP: REMOVING THE STIGMA

Let's talk about the elephant in the room—asking for help. For many caregivers, seeking assistance feels like admitting defeat, like waving a white flag in a battle you thought you could fight alone. You might fear judgment, thinking others will see you as inadequate or incapable of handling your responsibilities. It's as if an invisible scoreboard keeps track of your self-sufficiency, and asking for help feels like conceding points.

Cultural norms play a significant role here, too. In many societies, there's a stubborn belief that self-reliance is the gold standard, a badge of honor worn by those who never falter. But here's the thing: caregiving isn't a solo sport. It's a team effort, and sometimes, the most decisive move you can make is to reach out and say, "I could use a hand."

The benefits of seeking support are plentiful. Imagine having a lifeline tossed to you when you're feeling adrift. Emotional support from friends and family can be that lifeline, a buoy keeping you afloat amid the stormy seas of caregiving. It's the comforting voice on the other end of the phone, the reassuring hug at the end of a long day.

Beyond emotional support, professional advice can be invaluable, especially for navigating the financial challenges often accompanying caregiving. Whether it's assistance with budgeting, understanding insurance, or accessing community resources, professional guidance can illuminate paths you didn't even know existed. It's like having a GPS when you're lost in a maze of paperwork and expenses.

Overcoming the stigma of asking for help starts with education. The more you know about the resources available, the more empowered you feel to access them. Take the time to research support networks, both online and in your community. Many organizations offer a wealth of information and assistance, from respite care services to financial planning workshops.

Joining a support group can also be a game-changer. These groups provide a safe space to share experiences and reduce the isolation often accompanying caregiving. Picture a circle of chairs filled with people who get it. There's no judgment, just understanding and camaraderie.

Consider the story of Tom, a caregiver who initially struggled with asking for help. He felt he should be able to manage everything on his own, but the weight of caregiving was taking a toll on his mental health.

After much hesitation, Tom contacted a therapist, seeking guidance and support. Through therapy, he learned to navigate his emotions and developed strategies to cope with stress. The sessions became a sanctuary where he could unload his worries and gain perspective. Tom also discovered a local support group, where he met others facing similar challenges. Sharing stories and solutions with his peers made him realize he wasn't alone and that asking for help was not a sign of weakness but strength.

Stories like Tom's validate the power of seeking support. They remind us that reaching out is not a surrender, but a step toward resilience. You're not meant to carry the caregiving burden alone, so there's no shame in admitting you need assistance. So, take a deep breath, set aside the fear of judgment, and consider the resources available to you. Whether leaning on a friend, consulting a professional, or joining a support group, these connections can provide the support and understanding you need to continue your caregiving role with confidence and compassion.

BALANCING CAREGIVING AND CAREER: STRATEGIES FOR SUCCESS

Picture this: It's Monday morning, and you're gearing up for a day that feels like a grand juggling act. On one hand, you're managing a career that demands your focus and dedication. On the other, you're a caregiver with responsibilities that don't clock out at 5 pm. It's like balancing on a seesaw, with work and caregiving on either side, demanding your attention and energy.

For full-time caregivers, this balancing act can feel like navigating a maze without a map, where every turn leads to another set of challenges. The pressure to excel in both roles can be intense, leaving you feeling stretched thinner than a piece of overcooked spaghetti.

Managing time and energy between work and caregiving is no small feat. It's like having two full-time jobs with entirely different bosses, both expecting your undivided attention. Work deadlines loom, and caregiving tasks pile up, each vying for a top spot on your priority list.

It's easy to feel like you're constantly running on a treadmill—no matter how fast you go, the finish line never seems to appear. Add to this the expectations from employers who may not fully grasp the demands of caregiving and you've got a recipe for stress. Navigating employer expectations while fulfilling caregiving responsibilities can feel like a tightrope, where one misstep could make everything tumble.

So, how do you find balance in this whirlwind? It starts with setting realistic goals and priorities for both work and caregiving. Imagine your life as a garden, where each task is a plant needing care. You can't water them all at once, but prioritizing ensures each one gets what it needs to thrive. Identify what's most essential and focus your energy there. At work, this might mean breaking tasks into manageable chunks and tackling the most critical ones first.

For caregiving, it might involve scheduling essential activities and finding pockets of time for self-support. You don't have to do it all at once, and letting some things slide is okay. Remember, you're a human, not a superhero.

Utilizing flexible work arrangements can also be a game-changer. If your workplace offers options like remote work or flextime, take full advantage. It's like trading in a rigid schedule for a more adaptable one, allowing you to address caregiving needs without sacrificing your career. Don't hesitate to openly discuss your caregiving responsibilities with your employer.

Communication is key, and many employers are willing to accommodate when they understand the situation. Discuss potential adjustments to your work schedule, such as starting earlier or later, to better align with caregiving duties. Consider contacting human resources or employee assistance programs, which can provide additional support and resources.

Take the story of Karlie, a caregiver who successfully balanced her career as a project manager with her role as caregiver to her elderly father. When the demands of caregiving started to impact her work performance, Karlie knew she needed to find a solution. She approached her employer, explaining her situation and requesting flexible work hours.

To her relief, her employer was supportive, allowing her to adjust her schedule and work remotely when needed. This flexibility gave Karlie the breathing room she needed to manage her caregiving duties without compromising her career. With a supportive workplace and a clear plan in place, Karlie thrived in both roles, proving that balance is achievable with the right strategies.

Stories like Karlie's remind us that balancing work and caregiving is possible, even when it feels overwhelming. By setting priorities, communicating openly, and utilizing available resources, you can create a life where both your career and caregiving duties coexist harmoniously. It's about finding a rhythm that works for you, where each role complements the other rather than competes.

As you navigate this path, remember that it's okay to ask for help and to make adjustments along the way. You're not alone in this, and with the right tools, you can manage the demands of both work and caregiving with grace and resilience.

In the grand tapestry of life, balancing work and caregiving is a thread that weaves through our days, connecting us to the bigger picture.

9

CREATING A SUSTAINABLE CAREGIVING LIFESTYLE

Imagine waking up to a day that greets you like an old friend, with a sense of calm and predictability that makes even your morning coffee taste better. Creating your ideal caregiving day might sound like a fantasy, but with a sprinkle of planning and a dash of flexibility, it's more attainable than you might think.

Instead of feeling like you're being pulled in a thousand directions by invisible strings, you can orchestrate your day like a conductor leading a symphony, finding harmony between caregiving duties and personal needs. Now, before you roll your eyes and label this a pipe dream, let's delve into how we can make this a reality.

The first step in this orchestration is identifying your key caregiving tasks and priorities. Think of it like making a grocery list; you wouldn't leave the store without the essentials, right? Similarly, pinpoint the non-negotiables in your caregiving role. Maybe it's administering medication at specific times, coordinating appointments, or ensuring your loved one has a balanced meal.

You can prioritize and allocate your time more effectively by clearly identifying these crucial tasks. This doesn't mean every day will go off without a hitch. Still, it provides a roadmap, guiding you through the labyrinth of caregiving responsibilities with more clarity.

But what about you? Yes, you! Amidst all this planning, allocating time for personal and leisure activities is vital. Picture this as the cherry on top of your caregiving sundae. Whether it's a brisk walk around the block, a quick read of your favorite mystery novel, or a dance party in your kitchen, these moments are your recharge. They're the pause in your caregiving rhythm, giving you the energy to keep going. So, pencil them in, and treat them equally as any other task. Trust me, your sanity will thank you.

Let's talk about crafting that perfect day with a structured routine. Morning routines set the tone for everything that follows, much like the opening act in a theater production. Start with something that centers you, whether it's a few moments of deep breathing, a cup of coffee in silence, or a quick stretch to shake off the sleep.

These small rituals can transform your morning from a chaotic scramble into a tranquil prelude to the day. As the curtain rises on your day, you'll find yourself more grounded and ready to face the tasks ahead.

Evening wind-down rituals are just as crucial, acting like the closing scene that ties up the day with a neat bow. It's your chance to reflect, relax, and release the day's tensions. Maybe it's a warm bath, journaling about the day's highlights, or simply curling up with a cozy blanket and a favorite show. These rituals signal to your body and mind that it's time to shift gears and prepare for rest. They're not just about relaxation; they're a form of self-support that ensures you're recharged for tomorrow's encore.

Let's face reality: plans are great until life throws a curveball your way. That's where flexibility comes into play, like a safety net for your carefully choreographed day. As caregivers, we know unexpected demands are as common as misplaced socks in the laundry. A last-minute doctor's appointment or a sudden need for extra care can make your schedule tailspin. That's why building buffer time for transitions between tasks is essential. These little pockets of extra time act as cushions, absorbing the shocks of unpredictability and allowing you to adjust without derailing your day entirely.

Let me share a story about Claire, a caregiver who became a maestro of her own daily routine. Claire juggled a full-time job, caring for her mother with Alzheimer's, and maintaining a semblance of a personal life. Her secret? A structured routine that balanced work, caregiving, and family time. Mornings started with a short yoga session, setting a peaceful tone before diving into the day's tasks.

She used her lunch breaks to check in on her mother or run errands, ensuring her afternoons at work were focused and productive. Evenings were reserved for family dinners, a time to connect and unwind together. Claire's routine wasn't rigid but adaptable, allowing her to shift gears when caregiving demands changed. Her story proves the power of a well-crafted routine, proving that there's room for balance and fulfillment even amidst chaos.

Interactive Element: Designing Your Ideal Day

Take a moment to envision your ideal caregiving day. Grab a piece of paper or open a new document and create a simple schedule. Start with your non-negotiable caregiving tasks, then weave in pockets of personal time and leisure activities. Consider morning and evening rituals that ground and relax you.

Finally, add buffer time for those unexpected detours. Remember, this isn't set in stone—it's a living document that evolves with your needs. As you experiment with your routine, note what works and where adjustments are needed. This exercise isn't just about planning; it's about crafting a day that reflects your priorities and values, allowing you to thrive as a caregiver and an individual.

CULTIVATING A POSITIVE CAREGIVING ENVIRONMENT

Picture this: you walk into a room that's not just four walls and a ceiling but a sanctuary—a space that feels like a warm hug at the end of a long day. Creating a positive caregiving environment isn't just about aesthetics; it's about crafting a place where both you and your care recipient can thrive. Let's start with the physical space. Organizing caregiving areas for efficiency and comfort can be a game-changer. Imagine a kitchen where everything has its place and the chaos of clutter is but a distant memory.

By decluttering and organizing, you can create an environment where tasks feel less like a chore and more like a dance. Place frequently used items within easy reach and ensure that each caregiving tool has a designated spot. This saves time and reduces stress, turning your caregiving spaces into efficient hubs of productivity.

But efficiency is only part of the equation. Infusing these spaces with personal touches and positive reminders can transform them from functional to uplifting. Consider adding a splash of color with a vibrant painting or a cozy throw blanket that invites relaxation. Hang up a few cherished family photos or meaningful art pieces that spark joy and connection. These elements are like little beacons of happiness, guiding you through the toughest days with a smile.

Positive reminders, like a whiteboard with an inspiring quote or a sticky note with a heartfelt message, can act as daily affirmations, reinforcing the purpose and love that fuels your caregiving journey. It's about creating an environment that not only supports the tasks at hand but also nourishes the spirit.

Injecting positivity and joy into caregiving is more than a nice-to-have; it's a necessity. Imagine a gratitude wall adorned with uplifting quotes and photos that capture moments of laughter and love. Each glance at this wall is a reminder of the good amidst the challenges, a visual representation of the gratitude that powers your caregiving journey.

Setting up a cozy relaxation corner is another way to invite joy into your space. A plush chair, a soft blanket, and a shelf of favorite books create a nook where you can retreat for a moment of peace. This corner isn't just a physical space; it's a mental oasis, a place where you can recharge and reconnect with yourself. By intentionally creating these spaces, you cultivate an atmosphere of warmth and positivity that nurtures you and your care recipient.

Communication is the glue that holds a positive environment together. Open dialogue and understanding among caregivers and family members are crucial for fostering harmony. Picture this: regular family meetings where everyone gathers around the table, not just to discuss logistics, but to share feelings, concerns, and triumphs.

These meetings are a safe space for honest and empathetic conversations, where each voice is valued and every concern addressed. By encouraging open communication, you build a foundation of trust and collaboration, ensuring that everyone feels heard and supported. This dialogue extends beyond formal meetings; it's about creating a culture of openness where family members feel comfortable expressing their needs and preferences, knowing they'll be met with empathy and understanding.

Let me tell you about Sam, a caregiver who transformed his environment into a haven of comfort and accessibility. Sam's caregiving space was initially a maze of obstacles, with narrow hallways and cluttered surfaces challenging daily tasks. Determined to create a more supportive environment, he embarked on a redesign. He widened doorways for easier mobility, installed grab bars strategically, and rearranged furniture to create open pathways.

But Sam didn't stop at functionality; he infused the space with warmth by adding soft lighting, family photos, and calming colors. The result was a space that facilitated caregiving and provided a sense of peace and comfort for him and his care recipient. Sam's story illustrates the transformative power of a positive environment, showing how thoughtful changes can enhance both the caregiving experience and overall well-being.

In crafting a positive caregiving environment, you're not just arranging furniture or hanging pictures; you're creating a sanctuary that supports, uplifts, and inspires. It's about finding joy in the little things—a well-organized space, a cherished photo, or a heartfelt conversation. These elements come together to create an atmosphere that fosters connection, understanding, and resilience—an environment where both you and your care recipient can flourish.

Creating a sustainable caregiving lifestyle involves strategically planning your day around key caregiving tasks while intentionally scheduling personal moments and flexible routines for life's unpredictability. Establishing calming morning and/or evening rituals grounds caregivers, preparing them for daily responsibilities and replenishing their energy.

Crafting a positive caregiving environment through organized, personalized spaces and open family communication creates a nurturing sanctuary that supports both caregiver and care recipient in thriving together.

CONCLUSION

Well, my friend, we've reached the end of our journey through the winding roads of caregiving and burnout. It's been quite a ride, hasn't it? We've explored the nooks and crannies of this challenging landscape, shining a light on the hidden corners of stress and exhaustion. But more importantly, we've discovered the tools and strategies to navigate this terrain with grace, resilience, and a healthy dose of humor.

Throughout these pages, we've tackled the essential topics that every caregiver should have in their toolkit. We started by understanding the beast that is burnout, learning to recognize its sneaky symptoms and the importance of shifting our perspectives.

We delved into the art of building emotional resilience, crafting practical self-support strategies, and setting boundaries without drowning in guilt. We explored the power of enhancing relationships with our loved ones and our fellow caregivers. And we armed ourselves with tools for long-term resilience, from managing emotional stress to leveraging technology and creating a sustainable caregiving lifestyle.

But here's the thing: this book isn't just a collection of information and strategies. It's a vision, a purpose, a rallying cry for caregivers everywhere. When I set out to write this book, my goal was to empower you with actionable insights to prevent burnout and restore balance in your life, guilt-free. I wanted to show you that taking care of yourself isn't an optional extra; it's a necessity. And most importantly, I wanted to remind you that you're not alone in this journey.

So, what are the key takeaways from our time together? First and foremost, remember to recognize the signs of burnout. It's like learning to spot the red flags in a relationship—the earlier you catch them, the better. Secondly, embrace the power of small, simple strategies to manage stress. You don't need to realign your entire life; sometimes, the little things make the biggest difference. Thirdly, prioritize self-support like it's your job—because, in a way, it is. And lastly, don't be afraid to set boundaries. It's not about building walls; it's about creating a safe space for you to thrive.

Now, I know what you might be thinking: "This all sounds great, but can it really make a difference?" The answer is a resounding yes. Implementing these strategies has the potential to transform your caregiving experience, offering you a sense of hope and empowerment in your role. I've seen it happen in my own life and witnessed it in countless other caregivers' lives.

But here's the catch: it's not a one-and-done deal. Resilience and balance require continuous learning and adaptation. What works for you today might need some tweaking tomorrow. And that's okay. Embrace the journey, and trust that you have the tools to navigate whatever comes your way.

So, what's next? It's time to take action, my friend. Start small, start simple, but most importantly, start now. Integrate a new self-support routine into your day, set a boundary that protects your time, or reach out to a fellow caregiver for support. Remember, you have the tools, you have the knowledge, and you have the strength to make it happen.

But don't stop there. Reflect on your caregiving journey, celebrate your victories, and learn from your challenges. Engage with the community, whether it's joining a support group or hopping onto an online forum. There's power in shared experiences, in knowing that you're part of a tribe of resilient, compassionate, and downright awesome individuals.

As we close this book, I want to take a moment to express my gratitude and acknowledgment. I see you, I hear you, and I understand the challenges you face. Your dedication to your loved one and to your role as a caregiver is nothing short of heroic. And while the road ahead may have its twists and turns, know that you have the resilience, adaptability, and potential for growth and fulfillment in your caregiving journey.

Remember, this book is just the beginning. Keep learning, keep exploring, and keep seeking out resources that support your journey. Whether it's diving into another book, checking out a website, or connecting with an organization, there's a world of support out there, ready to help you thrive.

So, here's to you, my fellow caregiver. Here's to your strength, compassion, and unwavering commitment to making a difference in the lives of those you love. As you step into the future of your caregiving journey, know that you're not just surviving; you're thriving. With the tools and strategies you've gained from this book, I have no doubt that you'll continue to navigate this path with resilience, grace, and a healthy dose of laughter.

Keep shining, my friend. The world needs your light.

REFERENCES

Bandura, A. (n.d.). *Albert Bandura: Self-efficacy & agentic positive psychology.* PositivePsychology.com. https://positivepsychology.com/bandura-self-efficacy/

Cedar Hill Continuing Care Community. (n.d.). *The power of positive environments in care settings.* Cedar Hill Care. https://www.cedarhillcare.org/nurturing-hope-the-power-of-positive-environments-in-care-settings.html

Family Caregiver Alliance. (n.d.). *Support groups.* Family Caregiver Alliance. https://www.caregiver.org/connecting-caregivers/support-groups/

Forleo, M. (n.d.). *The ultimate guide to saying no (scripts included!)* Marie Forleo. https://www.marieforleo.com/blog/how-to-say-no-ultimate-guide

Harvey, A. (2017, November). *Silence to LOL* [Video]. TEDxAdelaide. https://www.ted.com/talks/annie_harvey_silence_to_lol

HomeChoice Home Care Solutions. (n.d.). *Effective communication techniques for caregivers.* HomeChoice Home Care. https://www.homechoicehomecare.com/careers-in-caring/communication-techniques-for-caregivers/

NAMI California. (n.d.). *The impact of gratitude on mental health.* National Alliance on Mental Illness. https://namica.org/blog/the-impact-of-gratitude-on-mental-health/

Neff, K. (n.d.-a). *Self-compassion practices: Cultivate inner peace and joy.* Self-Compassion. https://self-compassion.org/self-compassion-practices/

Neff, K. (n.d.-b). *Self-compassion.* Dr. Kristin Neff. https://self-compassion.org/

Orloff, J. (n.d.). *5 protection strategies for empaths.* Dr. Judith Orloff. https://drjudithorloff.com/5-protection-strategies-for-empaths/

Sacks, O. (1998). *The man who mistook his wife for a hat and other clinical tales* (Rev. ed.). Touchstone. (Original work published 1985)

Scott, E. (2023, August 9). *Self-efficacy: Why believing in yourself matters.* Verywell Mind. https://www.verywellmind.com/what-is-self-efficacy-2795954

TrackingTime. (n.d.). *How to master time blocking*. TrackingTime. https://trackingtime.co/productivity/guide-to-time-blocking.html

World Health Organization. (2019, May 28). *Burn-out an "occupational phenomenon": International classification of diseases*. World Health Organization. https://www.who.int/news/item/28-05-2019-burn-out-an-occupational-phenomenon-international-classification-of-diseases

ABOUT THE AUTHOR

Annie is a TEDx speaker, keynote speaker, mindfulness trainer and laughter yoga leader. This is the third book published by Annie.

Her other two titles are:

- **The Little Book of STILL: Calm for Busy Lives**
- **Young Hearts Wise Souls: Connecting Generations though Laughter, Mindfulness and More**

Annie is also the creator of The Giggle Game https://www.thestilleffect.com.au/gigglegame

You can find Annie at…

https://www.thestilleffect.com.au/

https://www.linkedin.com/in/annieharvey/

https://www.instagram.com/thestilleffect/

https://www.facebook.com/annieharveystill

https://www.tiktok.com/@annieharvey65?lang=en

Printed in Dunstable, United Kingdom